the beg[illegible]s guide to classic yoga

the beginner's guide to classic yoga

Frances Houlahan

Published by SILVERDALE BOOKS
An imprint of Bookmart Ltd
Registered number 2372865
Trading as Bookmart Ltd
Desford Road
Enderby
Leicester LE19 4AD

D&S Books Ltd
Cottage Meadow, Bocombe,
Parkham, Bideford
Devon, England
EX39 5PH

e-mail us at:-
enquiries@dsbooks.fsnet.co.uk

This edition printed 2002

ISBN 1-856056-92-9

Creative Director: Sarah King
Editor: Judith Millidge
Project editor: Clare Howarth-Maden
Photographer: Paul Forrester
Designer: 2H Design

Printed in Singapore

3 5 7 9 10 8 6 4 2

Contents

Introduction

The great science of Yoga encompasses every aspect of human psycho-physiology and the evolution of the body, mind and spirit. This book concentrates on establishing a solid foundation for Yoga practice by studying relaxation, poses, breath-work and meditation techniques.

Yoga originated in India many thousands of years ago. It is said that men and women known as *rishis,* or seers, used the natural cycles of nature to observe the effects of the seasons on the human mind and body. They studied the animals in the forests and discovered many cures for various human conditions. These scholars shared their knowledge and, over time, more information was discovered about the qualities of human life and how to maintain a healthy body and a peaceful mind. In about the second century AD, this knowledge was written down for posterity in Sanskrit by the great seer Patanjali. His manuscript provides a guide to advanced Hatha Yoga known as *Hatha Yoga Padipika*.

The word 'Yoga' comes from the ancient Sanskrit root *yug* or *yuj*, meaning 'union'. Here the union applies to the body, mind and

breath, so that during your lifetime you are able to guide your own destiny with a healthy mind, a flexible body and a steady breath in all conditions.

Yoga is a physical and mental discipline that has been practised for thousands of years. As it evolved, various cultures developed that specialised in specific aspects of Yoga, depending on the individual nature of the student. It owes much to the guru-and-disciple tradition that continues to this day. The Yoga practised in the West has its roots in the great guru lineage, which preserved and passed on the knowledge to successive generations.

The philosophy of Yoga stresses that the human body is a magnificent creation of nature, born to experience the greatness of the world. The body is therefore the temple of the spirit, and when the body, mind and breath are in balance and harmony, this inner light can shine forth and illuminate the shadows of the world. Yoga philosophy believes that the spirit is infinite, and that the true nature of all beings is peaceful and blissful. Therefore the goal of Yoga practice is to preserve this peace.

The different types of Yoga were designed to nurture specific qualities in the students, and the gurus based their teachings on what would best honour and nurture the spiritual awakening of the individual's nature. Yoga is therefore not just physical exercise, but a complete, holistic philosophy, a way of life that encourages evolution on all levels of consciousness.

Yoga philosophy is quite emphatic about the correct state of mind required if any progress is to be made. There must be absolutely no desire for competition or any expectation of achievement. The process of Yoga practice is a journey, and revelations and releases will occur naturally in your mind and body as you become aware that your everyday senses and perceptions are being heightened and expanded. In this sense, although students do not set out to achieve anything, they experience a great deal through the inner realms of consciousness.

The wonderful benefits of Yoga begin immediately, as the body softens and the mind becomes clear and calm. Yoga maintains all

the systems of the body, both inside and out — the mental and the physical. It encourages a quiet sense of inner knowledge and psychological stability that magnify perceptions of one's life.

Ordinary exercise is outwardly projected, which debilitates the natural storehouse of energy within the body. The inward direction of Yoga, which is created naturally by the stillness and slowness of the poses and measured breathing, develops a natural composure of harmony and balance to the nervous system. At the same time, all of the muscles, ligaments and tendons of the body begin to lengthen comfortably, without stress, and the joints become lubricated.

All of the poses have a profound effect deep inside the body, bathing and soaking all of the organs and glands as the body irrigates itself with natural fluids. You may notice that you need less sleep because your energy is boosted, and that your digestive system becomes healthier and more efficient. When this occurs, you will convert food into nutrition for the body more easily, which increases your vitality.

As the balancing processes continue and your practice intensifies, you will begin to notice that your body really wants to experience the bliss of Yoga. Old, unhealthy habits will begin to fade away. When you reach this level of awakening, there are many more aspects of Yoga to explore. You may choose to attend a class, where you will be able to share your experiences with other Yoga students and seek answers from the teacher to some of your questions.

It is important to remember that Yoga poses are not aerobic exercises as such, but are specific prescriptions for achieving maximum health and supreme physical condition. Each pose causes chemical changes in the body and the mind because of the effects on the endocrine system. As you become more familiar with Yoga practice, you will become extremely sensitive to the subtle and wonderful changes occurring within your body.

The main types of Yoga

Ashtanga Vinyasa Yoga

This is an energetic series of poses that flow together and become more challenging as the muscles and joints gain flexibility and strength. The mind is focused on the breathing, Ujayyi breath, which encourages the body to develop heat to boost the release of toxins from deep within the tissue cells. This is a dynamic Yoga therapy. It is a combination of Hatha and Raja yoga.

Bhakti Yoga

A person who chooses to practice Bhakti Yoga – 'the Yoga of Devotion' – will be concerned with the path of selfless service. They will be involved with humanitarian activities without seeking reward or approval. This develops compassion and opens the heart chakra.

Hatha Yoga

(*Ha* means sun; *tha* means moon.) This Yoga involves mastering the poses (*asanas*) and controlling the breath (*pranayama*) using various techniques. It is this type that has been modified for Western bodies. Hatha Yoga balances the cosmic energies of the sun and moon in the mind and body, creating a harmonious flow of *prana* (life force).

Kundalini Yoga

A very subtle, yet powerful, practice that deals with the psychic, dormant energy called *kundalini* which is stored at the base of the spine like a coiled serpent waiting to wake up. By concentrating on this energy, it becomes revitalised and moves upwards through the chakras, increasing clarity of consciousness and perception.

Raja Yoga

Royal Yoga – the 'Yoga of the Mind' – requires the aspirant to delve into the layers of the mind using observation and concentration to lead to deeper levels of meditation. The classic pose for Raja Yoga is the seated lotus, which encourages stillness in the mind and develops great peace and contentment.

Ashtanga Yoga — the traditional stages = the eight limbs of Yoga

The following stages or steps are used to guide the student through the physical, mental and spiritual levels towards self-realisation, or *samadhi*. They may occur separately or simultaneously during your life and practice.

The *Yamas* (*Yama* means abstention or restraint) are five ethical disciplines that guide us to look inwards and begin to take an inventory of our inner reality. The *Niyamas* relate to individual concepts, such as the quality of life and relationships with all beings in the world.

The first limb

Yamas

1. *Ahimsa*: non-violence. Do not kill any living creature. Control internal anger and violent thoughts or actions. Embrace all creation with love and respect.
2. *Satya*: truth. Live your truth and look within to see the oneness of all life. Do not falsify your existence.
3. *Asteya*: non-stealing. Do not envy the possessions or status of others. Be content in the here and now.
4. *Bramacharya*: preserve the creative life force. Some people interpret this as celibacy, which would not be appropriate in a loving relationship. It guides us to respect our natural energies.
5. *Aparigraha*: non-possessiveness. Do not hoard possessions or take more than you need. Do not gather clutter in your life as it is a reflection of mental clutter.

The second limb

Niyamas

1. *Saucha*: purity. Try to develop pure habits of mind and body.
2. *Santosa*: contentment. Cultivate contentment and tranquillity in the mind.
3. *Tapas*: self-illumination. Live your life with inspiration and purpose.
4. *Svadhyaya:* self-study. The continued education of the nature of self.
5. *Isvara Pranidhana*: Dedication and surrender to your god.

The third limb

***Asana*:** poses. This third limb of Yoga is about learning to hold the poses in stillness, with a calm mind and smooth breath, to encourage mental equilibrium.

The fourth limb

Pranayama: breath control. Develop conscious breathing with a long, smooth flow of breath to keep the attention of the mind calm.

The fifth limb

Pratyahara: withdrawal of the senses. The mind naturally turns inwards during Yoga practice, which brings the outwardly directed senses under control.

The sixth limb

Dharana: concentration. Mental focus is achieved through the poses and breath-work. There are specific methods that help to develop concentration.

The seventh limb

Dhyana: contemplation or meditation. The mind dwells in its own field of consciousness and the self observes the process.

The eighth limb

Samadhi: enlightenment or self-realisation. The culmination of practice and where the boundaries of illusion and duality dissolve. In this state, true Yoga, or union, is experienced in the form of cosmic consciousness which is, by its very nature, indescribable.

The ancient teachings use a beautiful story to illustrate the unfolding of the spiritual nature of humans. They describe the lotus plant, which grows in murky water, sending its roots deep into the mud, which holds firm in the churning water. Then the stem grows steadily upwards and pierces the surface, where the lotus blooms and offers its petals to the sun. We are also growing towards the light — the spiritual light that illuminates the entire cosmos.

The chakra system

For centuries, *yogis* (teachers) have taught the importance of the chakras and the energies stored within them. The Sanskrit word literally means 'spinning wheel', 'circle' or 'vortex of invisible cosmic energies'. Like the wind, these energies are invisible, yet we can see their effects just as the effects of the wind are evident in the rustling of the leaves on a summer day or in a tropical hurricane. The chakras interpenetrate the physical body from the subtle bodies and are represented by the master glands of the endocrine system. There are seven major chakras and many smaller ones; through them, crisscrossing all over the body, are the 72,000 nadis. The nadis are a network of pathways or meridians that carry the vital life force through the chakras and the subtle bodies in much the same way as the physical nervous system sends electrical impulses and information to all of the cells in the body and back to the brain. This vital life force is called *prana,* and the *yogis* learned how to manipulate its flow through various poses. The three main nadis are the moon channel at the left nostril, the sun channel at the right nostril and the central fire channel through the spinal cord.

Each chakra represents qualities inherent in a person that may be active or dormant. It is said that if a chakra becomes blocked or stagnant, then an illness may occur in the physical area relating to it; by releasing the trapped energy, the physical blockage may also be released. Each chakra has particular qualities relating to human nature, as well as colour vibration and a sound or mantra. Great studies have been done on the chakra system and it can be extremely complex.

All of the Yoga poses affect the chakras and help to keep the energies flowing freely. Beginning at the base of the spine and moving upwards to the crown of the head, the dormant energies are slowly awakened to release the full potential of the human experience and culminate at the thousand-petalled lotus above the crown. The chakras are likened to the unfolding of the lotus flower as it strives towards the light; in the same way, the ascending consciousness of a human being strives towards cosmic awareness.

During meditation, you may choose to focus on one chakra and experience the energy and vibrations stored within it. Use the diagram as a guide to focus on the bodily area and visualise or wear the colour of that centre.

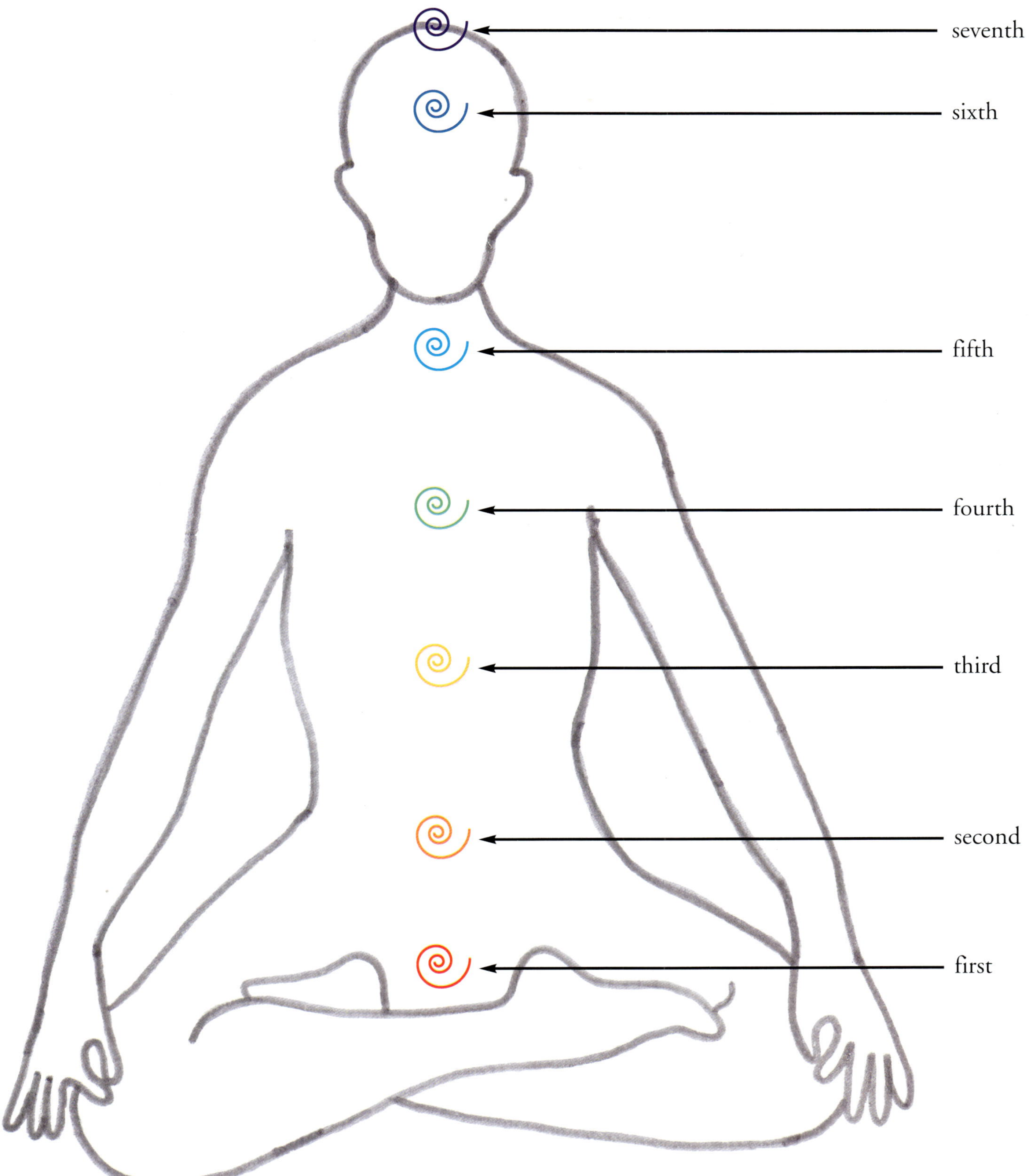
seventh
sixth
fifth
fourth
third
second
first

A guide to the chakras

First chakra

Muladhara: root system
Area of the body: perineum
Element: earth
Gland: adrenals / reproductive system
Colour: red
Quality: survival

Second chakra

Svadhisthana: sweetness
Area of the body: sacral plexus
Element: water
Gland: reproductive system / adrenals
Colour: orange
Quality: desire

Third chakra

Manipura: lustrous
Area of the body: solar plexus
Element: fire
Gland: pancreas, adrenals
Colour: yellow
Quality: willpower

Fourth chakra

Anahata: harmony
Area of the body: heart
Element: air
Gland: thymus
Colour: green
Quality: compassion

Fifth chakra

Vishuda: purity
Area of the body: throat centre
Element: sound through air
Gland: thyroid, hypothalamus
Colour: sky blue
Quality: communication of truth

Sixth chakra

Ajna: cognition, perception
Area of the body: forehead, third eye
Element: light
Gland: pineal
Colour: indigo
Quality: intuition, imagination

Seventh chakra

Sahasrara: thousand-petalled lotus
Element: thought
Gland: pituitary
Colour: violet, purple
Quality: bliss, all-knowing

During your Yoga practice, notice which areas of the body feel stuck and observe which chakra is associated with that area. You might like to include some specific poses or stretches that bring comfort and ease to that part of your being.

Getting started

You only need a small amount of space to practise Yoga — just enough space to lie down or stretch, so there should be room in even the smallest home.

Choose a quiet and peaceful place to practise Yoga, and make sure that you will not be disturbed by the phone or other people. Try to do this regularly and ensure that your privacy is respected. If possible, practise at the same time every day.

The very best times to practise Yoga and meditation are at sunrise and sunset, when the energies of the Earth are stable with the planetary lights. This is not always possible in our busy, modern schedules, so use your intuition about when is best for you. Here are some guidelines that will help you to establish your routine. You will quickly learn to make any necessary modifications to suit your individual nature and lifestyle.

1 Always make sure that your stomach is empty of solid food. Never practise Yoga with a full stomach. If you feel hungry before your practice, drink some diluted fruit juice or warm milk with a little honey in it. Practise Yoga before breakfast or at least two hours after a main meal.

2 Choose the surface that you feel comfortable working on. You will need a mat or folded blanket that is thick enough to protect your spine and joints from bruising. If you already have an exercise mat, it may be perfect for Yoga. You might need a cushion to use as a neck support during relaxation or other floor poses.

3 Make sure that the room you are working in is warm and well ventilated, but not draughty. During the relaxation sequence, have a blanket to cover your body with to maintain an even temperature, as you will loose heat during times of physical stillness.

4 Wear clothing that is loose and comfortable, so that your body feels free during the poses. In winter, a tracksuit is perfect, and in summer, a leotard or shorts and T-shirt. It is important that the abdominal area and ribcage are free to expand naturally and are not restricted by tight clothing.

Burning incense or an essential oil may help in relaxation.

5 If you are pregnant, consult your physician before beginning Yoga practice.

6 Never force your body beyond your 'comfort zone'. You will learn what this is when you begin to warm up and notice where the tension and fatigue are most evident. Your body will change daily, and with the seasons, and it is important that you respond gently and patiently to it.

7 In the beginning, your aim is to master the poses very gently without strain, so that your body feels free, yet experiences a new level of release. This feeling of freedom and lightness begins immediately with your practice.

8 During the poses, your breathing will become deep and regular, which is the natural Yogic breath. Never hold your breath, but allow each exhalation to be deep and smooth. Each time you practise a pose, your body will become more relaxed and will release old holding patterns, so relax by using the smooth rhythm of your breathing. Never force, push or strain your body beyond the natural comfort zone. Practise to encourage the release, and not the increase, of tension.

9 If you feel tired, hot or dizzy, go into the relaxation pose and focus on smooth breathing while your body stabilises and rests for at least five minutes. Always begin and end your practice in this pose for at least five minutes.

10 Yoga practice will help all conditions, but we are all unique and carry different levels of resistance to change, so if you have a medical condition, or are taking medication, it is wise to consult your physician for advice before commencing.

11 During the practice, you may wish to play some relaxing music to help your mind become calm and peaceful. If you find your eyes closing when you are holding the poses, this is a natural progression towards meditation and is to be welcomed. A scented candle will encourage a relaxed mind, as will burning incense or essential oil.

12 A little Yoga goes a long way. Remember to be easy and gentle in your working. A simple guide to assist this process is: inhale as you prepare to move and exhale when you arrive.

During a practice, it is helpful to sip warm water, which will facilitate the internal cleansing process and also dilate the pathways for the easy transition of whatever substances the body wants to move around. At the end of your practice, you may choose to meditate or spend more time in the relaxation pose.

Soothing music may help you to relax in preparation for Yoga.

Caution: if you have any medical condition, or are taking prescribed medication, consult your physician before beginning your practice.

Warming up

Warming your body before practising the poses is absolutely essential to prevent strain or injuries occurring. Even the easy poses have a deep effect on the internal organs, muscles, glands and joints, and the warm-up sequence prepares your body for the work to come. It is important to emphasise that you must never push or force your body during the practice. If you experience any physical discomfort the following day, it is a warning that you have over-worked your body. Always listen to the nuances of your body during a practice and proceed accordingly. The following points will guide you.

1 Always practise some warm-up stretches to prepare your body for deeper release work.
2 If you only have ten minutes to spare for practice, use a selection from the warm-up only.
3 Always begin and end your practice in the relaxation pose.
4 Work gently, breathe evenly and enjoy the wonder of being . . .

Warm-up sequence

Relaxation pose

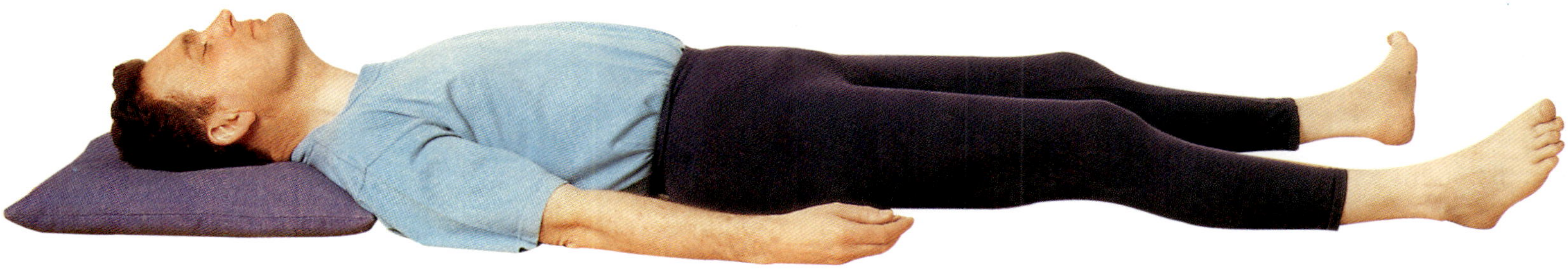

1. Lie on a mat on your back and place your feet wide apart, with your toes flopping sideways. Place a small pillow under your neck for support. Rest your arms at your sides or place your palms over your stomach to experience deep abdominal breathing. Cover yourself with a blanket if you feel cold. Allow your body to become very still and simply enjoy this natural process of relaxation.

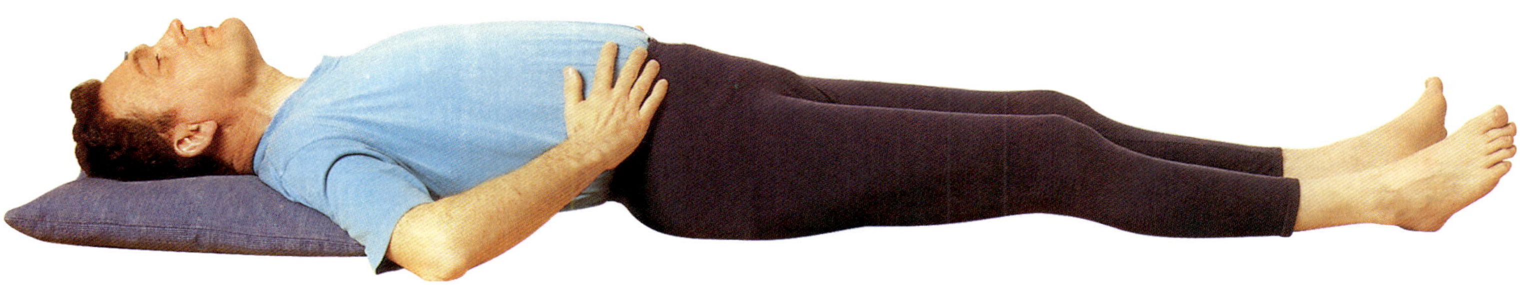

2. Practise abdominal breathing, which will keep your busy mind occupied and prepare you for a calm and peaceful practice.

At the end of the relaxation pose, stretch your arms and legs to stimulate your circulation and prepare for your next work.

Breath techniques *Pranayama*

Breathing techniques, or *pranayama*, the control of *prana* (life force), are paramount to Yoga practice, and have a supreme effect on the mind and body. This inward focus on the quality and ratio of the breaths creates a profound shift of consciousness. The mind is usually focused externally, on the mundane world, so its energies are directed outwards. When attention and awareness are bought to focus on the breathing process and the sounds of the breath itself, something metaphysical happens. Your own personal experience will shed more light on this subject.

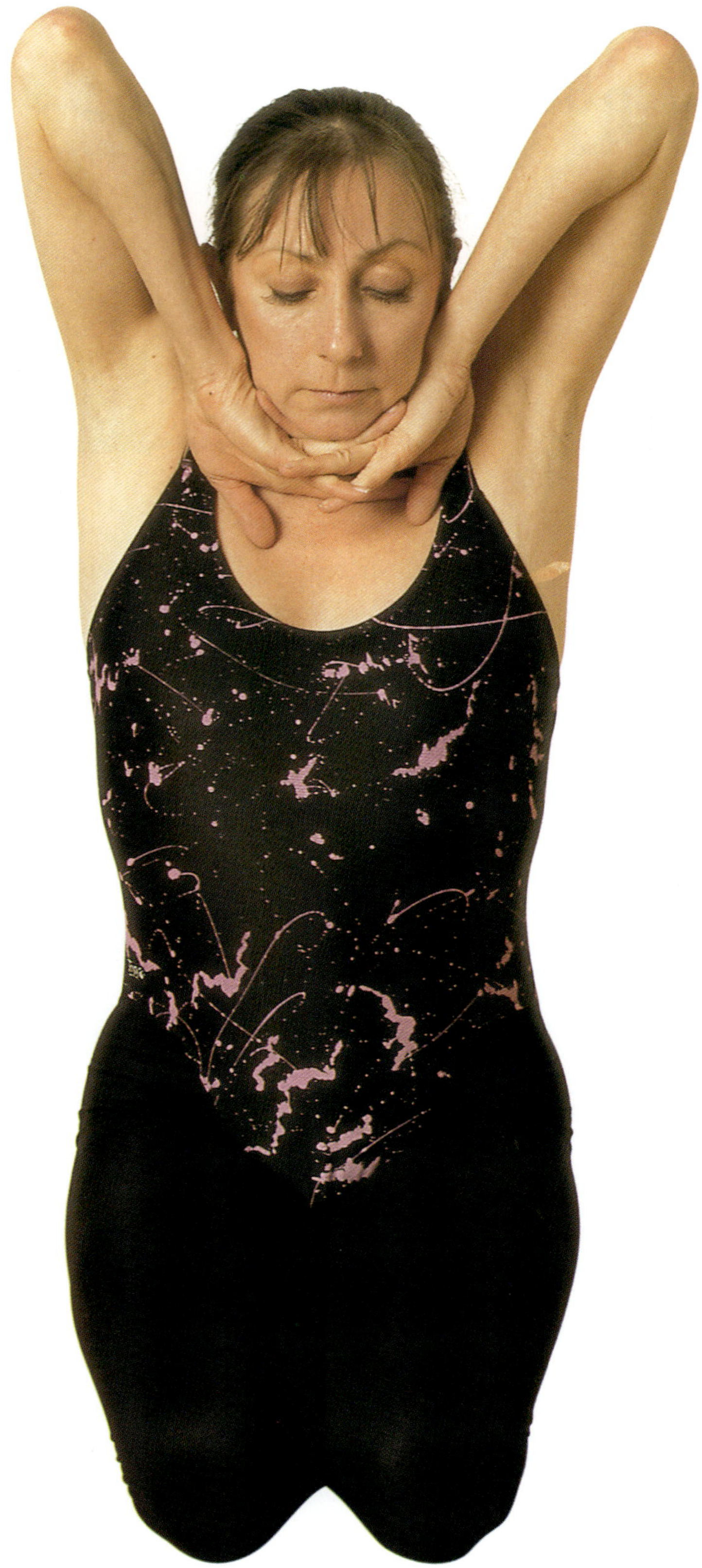

Abdominal breathing: Yoga complete breath

This breath is usually practised in the relaxation pose, and can naturally be incorporated into other poses as your awareness expands.

Bring your attention to the whole area beneath your ribcage and down to your hip bones. Gradually deepen your exhaling breath and feel all of the muscles in this area make a slow, firm contraction, consciously squeezing the muscles towards your naval centre. On the inhalation, allow this area to expand slowly, as far as it wants to go, feeling very round and full. Slowly exhale again. This is one complete breath. Try 21 of these, letting your mind follow the process of expansion and contraction, knowing that each conscious breath is bringing your mind to a calm and quiet place, preparing you for the practice to come. This breath pacifies and calms the central nervous system.

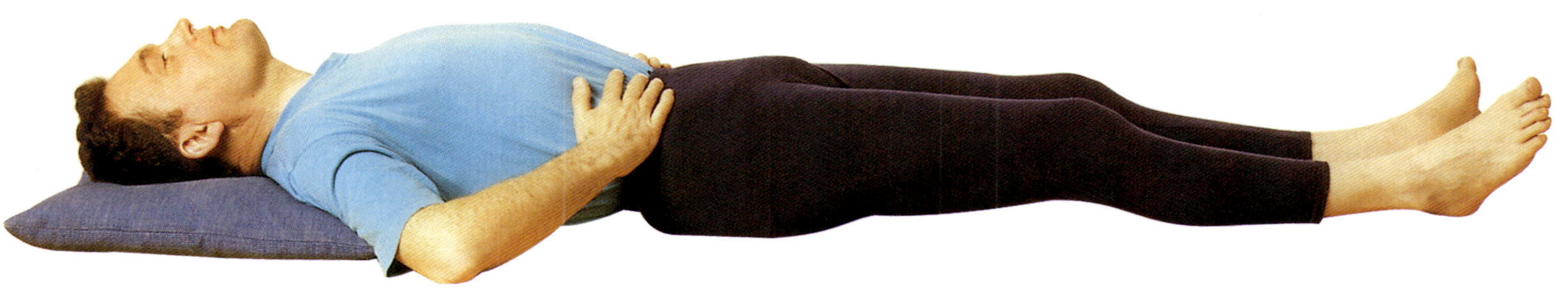

Simple breath

This powerful, yet simple, breath stretches the muscles between the ribs, keeping them flexible so that your ribcage can expand and contract easily and evenly during respiration. You will also feel that tightness in the shoulder and chest area is released when you use this breath, due to the raising and lowering of the arms.

1. Kneel or sit in a comfortable pose on your mat or chair and clasp your fingertips together, placing them under your chin.

2. As you press your chin down into your fingers and raise your elbows as high as you can, inhale deeply and evenly through your nostrils and count one, two, three. Hold in the breath for a few seconds.

3. Exhale deeply and evenly through your open mouth, making a sighing noise, and count to three, letting your head stretch backwards and bringing your elbows together. Begin with 9 breaths and increase them gradually to 21. You may also choose to increase your lung capacity by extending the breath count, e.g., inhale for four counts, then five or six, and the same when exhaling.

Alternate-nostril breath

This breath balances the energies of the central nervous system and is particularly beneficial for people with bronchial conditions or asthma. Sit in a comfortable pose and lift your spine as high as you can. This is important because of the flow of energy through the spinal canal. You may also practise this breath whilst seated in a chair.

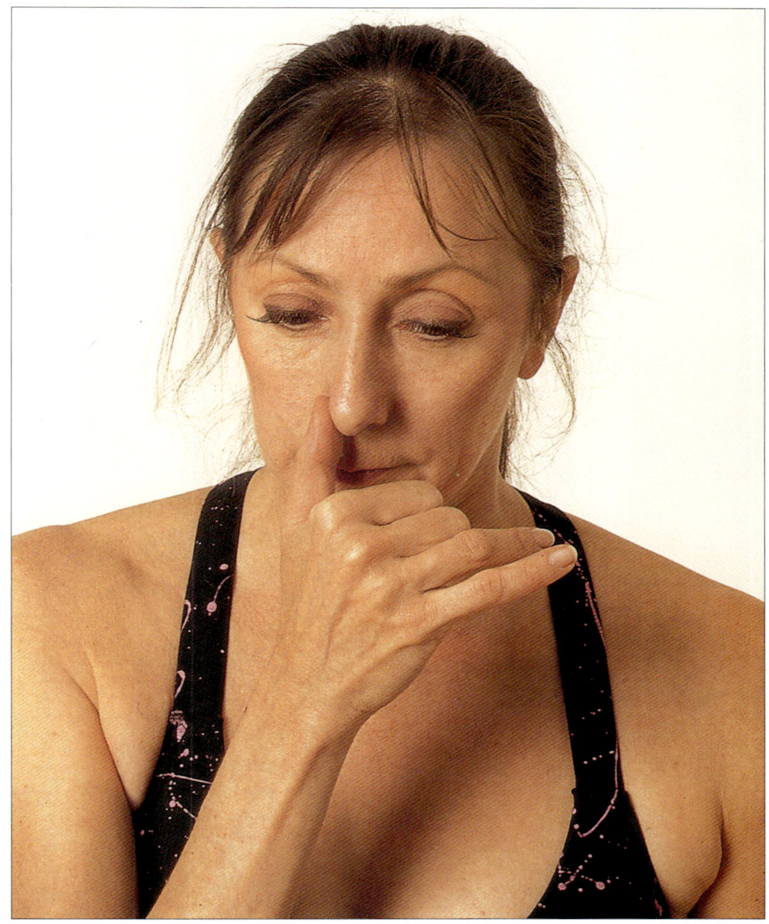

2. Close your right nostril with your thumb and exhale to the left side.

1. Make a soft fist with your right hand and extend your thumb and last two fingers.

3. Inhale deeply through the left side for a count of three and close the left nostril with two fingers. Exhale to the right side for a count of six.

4. Inhale on the right side for a count of three and close the right nostril with your thumb.Exhale on left side for a count of six. This is one round of the alternate-nostril breath. Begin with six rounds and increase gradually.

Supine twist

1. Inhale. Bend your knees, with your feet flat on the mat, and place your hands behind your head.

2. Exhale deeply and roll both legs to the left side, creating a lumbar twist. Hold this for as long as it feels comfortable.

3. Inhale and pull your legs up.

4. Exhale, with your legs to the other side. You may repeat this if you want to stretch your spine further.

Colon massage: head-to-knee squeeze

This is a wonderful pose to tone the abdominal organs and keep the colon healthy. The right side tones the ascending colon and the left side the descending colon. It also gently stretches and lengthens the spine.

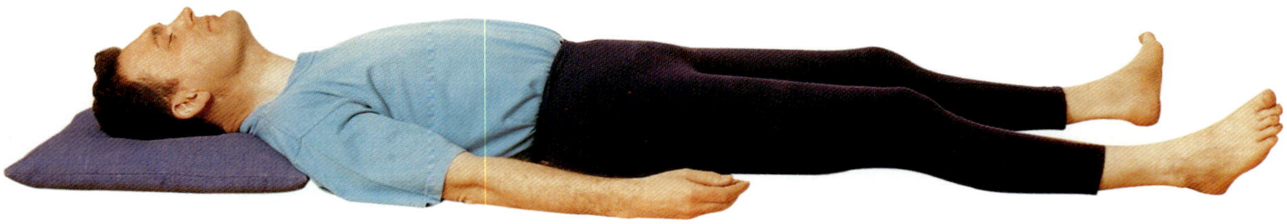

1. Lie flat on your back, with your feet together.

2. Inhale and squeeze your right knee towards your right shoulder.

3. Exhale and slowly raise your head towards your knee. Breathe softly, then release your leg and head and repeat on the other side.

Butterfly pose

This simple pose has many benefits, including freeing the hip joints, lengthening the spine, energising the kidneys and releasing pressure from the abdominal cavity. In the beginning, you may find stiffness in the hip area, but this will ease with practice.

1. Sit tall and bring the soles of your feet together.

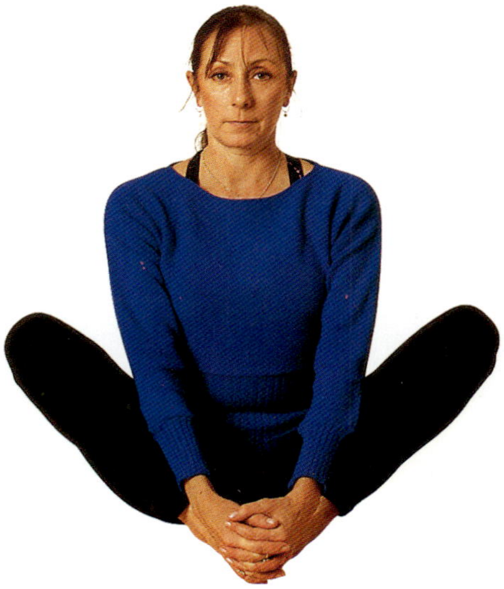

2. Hold onto the outsides of your feet and pull your knees inwards, towards your chin.

3. Inhale deeply and, as you exhale, press your knees towards the floor. Hold this for a few breaths, then repeat a few times.

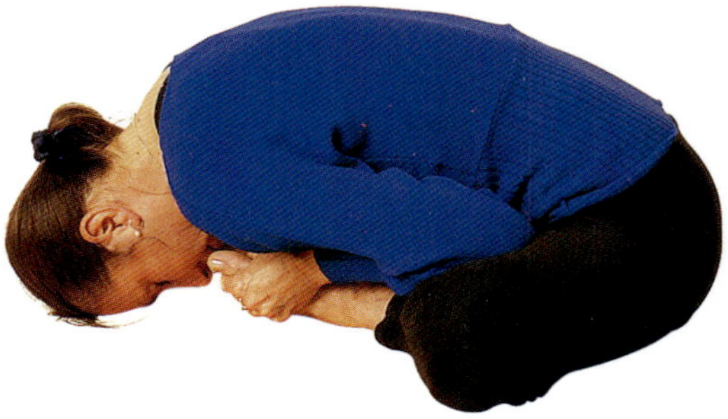

4. Now, keeping your spine long, fold yourself forwards and bring your head towards your toes. Relax completely and allow the down force of gravity to bring you forwards.

Shoulder stretch

This stretch works the shoulders, arms, chest, spine and the sides of the body.

1. Clasp your fingers together and press your palms forward as you exhale.

2. Raise your arms above your head and inhale.

3. Keep pushing upwards for as long as you can, using deep breathing. If you want more work, take your arms backwards as far as they will reach. Shake and shrug your shoulders a few times when you have finished this stretch.

Head rolls/neck stretch

1. Sit on your mat in a comfortable position and lengthen your spine.

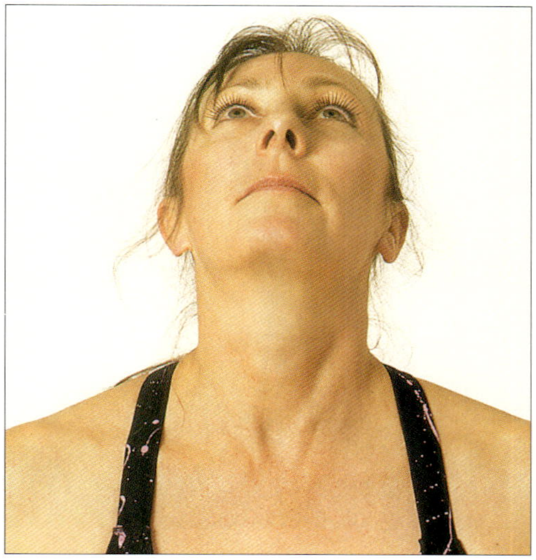

2. Inhale and lower your chin to the middle of your chest.

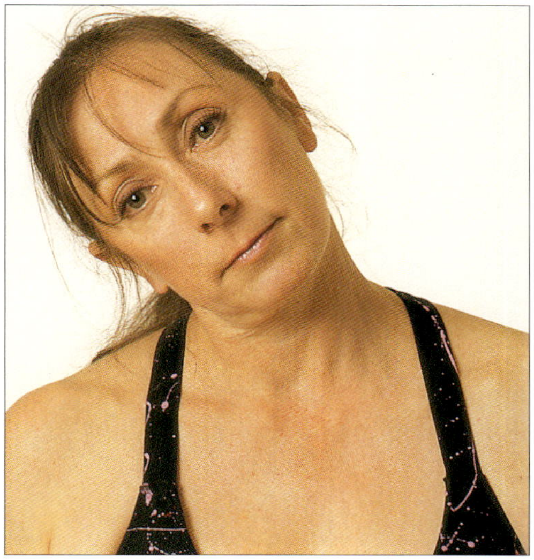

3. Slowly roll your head to one side.

4. Then roll it back and to the other side.

5. Return your chin to your chest.

6. Continue rolling in large and smooth circles, about three times.

7. Then reverse and repeat on the other side.

Caution: this movement must be slow and sensitive to the delicate nature of the neck nerves and vertebrae, so listen to your body and work accordingly.

Seated side stretch

1. Sit in a cross-legged pose on your mat and place your hands behind your head, with your fingers clasped together to support your neck. Keep your elbows high and pulled back to prevent your body from drooping forwards.

2. Inhale and exhale, bringing your right elbow to rest on your right knee. Stay here for a few breaths as you feel the left side of your body begin to soften and release.

3. Inhale deeply to come back up.

4. Then exhale to the left side, placing your left elbow on your left knee.

5. Return to the starting pose as you inhale.

6. As your side stretch becomes more flexible, try resting your elbow on the floor beside your knee to experience deeper work.

Single-leg lifts

1. Lie back on your mat, with your feet together.

2. Inhale and bend your right knee, raising it towards your chest.

3. Exhale and straighten your leg as much as you can.

4. Inhale and bend your leg into your chest again, then exhale to lower your leg onto the mat.

5. Repeat on the left side. Practise this sequence three times on each side.

Don't worry if your knee isn't straight yet: that will come with more practice. This sequence strengthens the spine muscles, maintains mobility of the hips and knees and keeps the leg muscles toned.

Double-leg lift

This repeats the previous sequence, but with both legs together.

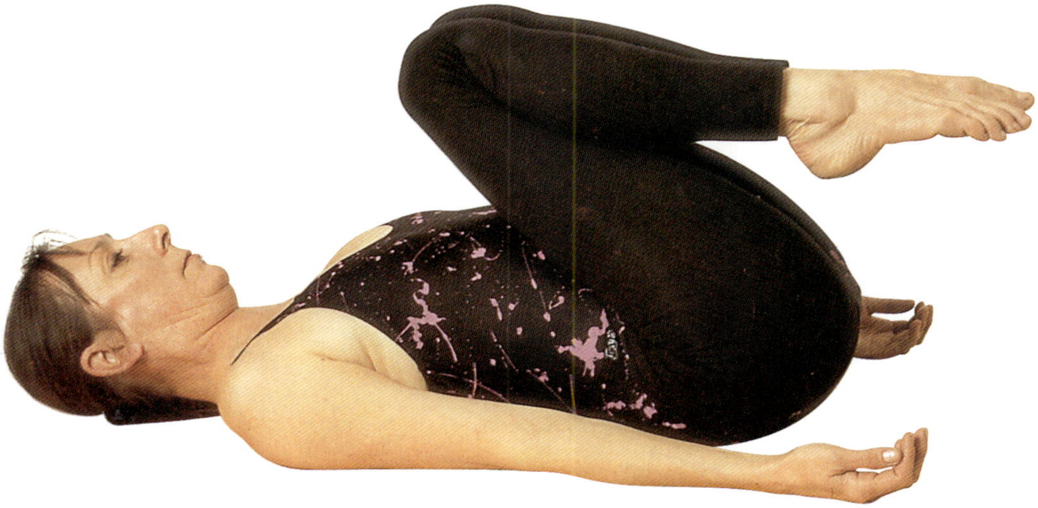

1. Inhale and bend your knees to your chest.

2. Exhale and extend your legs upwards.

Caution: during the double-leg lift, the lower spine is working strongly to support the weight of your legs, so it is important to keep your lower-back and waist area pressed firmly into your mat. If you feel your back beginning to arch during the lifting, stop. Continue with the single-leg lifts for a few more weeks until your back and stomach muscles are stronger, then resume the double lifts.

Sitting half-leg-forward bend

1. Sit on the mat with both legs straight out in front.

2. Bend your left knee and place your left foot flat on the inside of your right thigh. Raise your arms above your head and lift your body as high as you can.

3. Inhale. Lean forwards and hold your right ankle or foot. Allow the natural weight of your body to create the stretch comfortably. Hold the pose and breathe deeply and slowly. You will feel the stretch occurring at the back of your right leg. Repeat on the other side.

To come out of the pose, raise your arms and stretch upwards. You will eventually bring your head to rest on your knee, but this may take some time to achieve. This pose stretches the hamstring muscles and the lower spine and brings blood to the front of the brain.

Cobra stretch

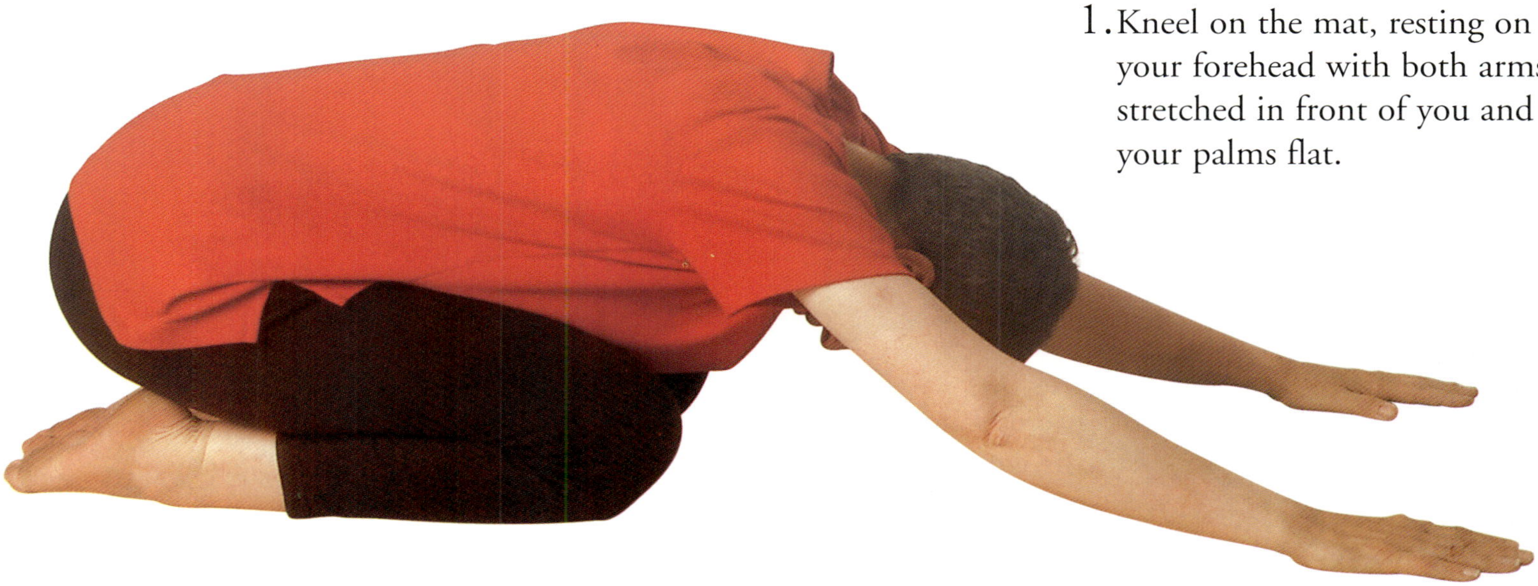

1. Kneel on the mat, resting on your forehead with both arms stretched in front of you and your palms flat.

2. Inhale and raise yourself up onto your knees, round your back and let your head hang downwards. Hold this pose for a few breaths; you will feel a gentle stretching between your shoulder blades.

3. Exhale, lowering your hips to the mat. You can bend your elbows slightly if this feels more comfortable.

4. Inhale and slowly raise your chin upwards. Hold this pose for three or four breaths, keeping your knees on the mat. This gives a strong flex to the lower back and expands the chest fully while also working the arms and shoulders.

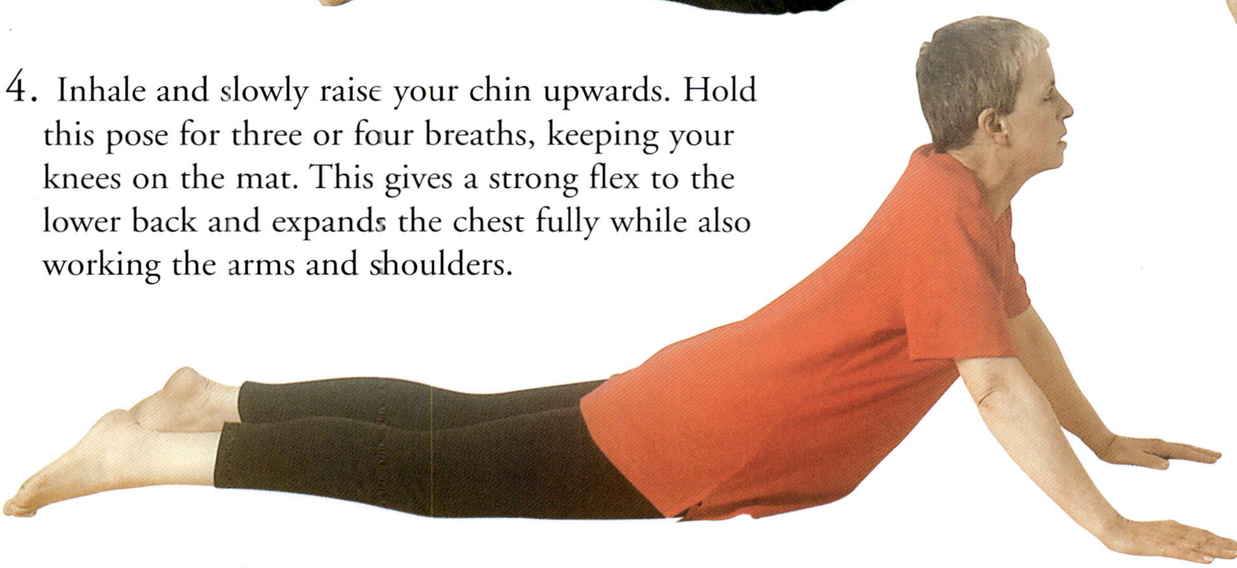

Reverse the sequence and return to the starting position to rest. Repeat two or three times.

When you have learned this pose and feel ready to increase your work, try to straighten your knees to balance on your hands and insteps only. This gives a wonderful stretch to the abdominal muscles.

Spinal curl

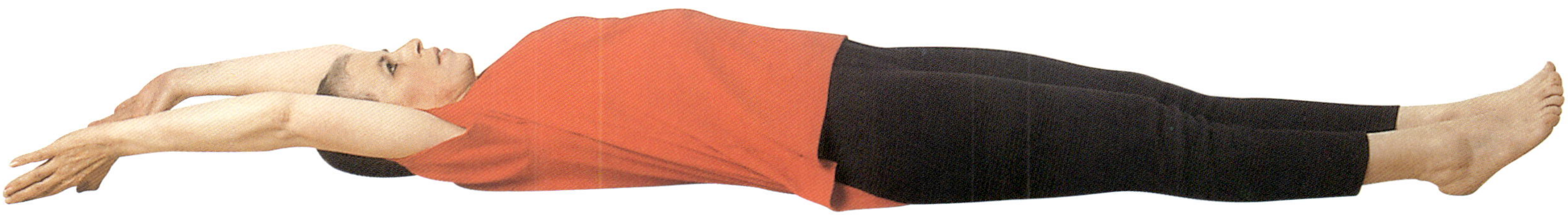

1. Stretch out on your back and raise your arms above your head. Lengthen your body as much as you can.

2. Inhale. Stretch your arms and legs.

3. Exhale and raise your body, bend your knees, hold your heels and rest your head on your knees. Really hug your body close to your legs.

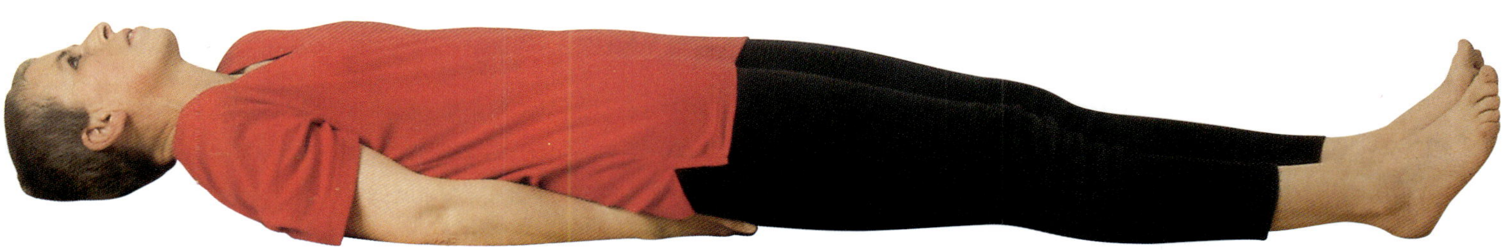

Lie back and relax for a moment and then repeat the sequence a few more times.

This simple stretch is really beneficial for the spine and helps the body to release tension.

Deep shoulder stretch

You may do this pose sitting, kneeling or standing, and it is an excellent way to release tension from the upper body.

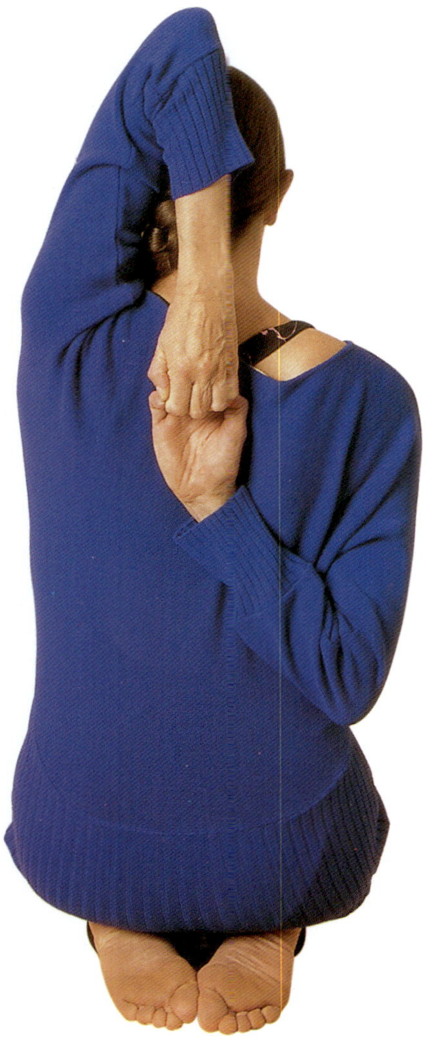

1. Stretch one arm behind your back and slide your hand up as high as it will reach between your shoulder blades. Place your other arm behind your head and try to hold your fingers. This may be hard to achieve the first time.

2. Hold the pose for a minute while breathing smoothly, then repeat on the other side. During the pose, you can press your head back slightly to increase the opening stretch of the shoulder. Repeat on the other side.

When people experience this pose for the first time, they are amazed at the difference in mobility between their right and left sides. Yoga encourages the use of the non-dominant side of the body to maintain a healthy equilibrium throughout the muscular system.

Chest expansion

1. Sit comfortably on a mat and place your arms behind your waist, holding your elbows in your palms. Lift the front of your chest and hold the pose using deep breathing. Change your hands over and hold the opposite elbows for a few more breaths.

2. To deepen this stretch, place your palms and fingers together behind your waist; try to place your palms together flat. This is very good for the wrists, which can hold a lot of tension. Squeeze your elbows further backwards to deepen the stretch.

3. These poses prepare you to hold your fingers behind your back, as in the previous shoulder stretch.

The poses – *asanas*

Mountain pose

This is a basic standing pose to develop awareness of correct posture, with the weight balanced evenly over the feet. Choose different arm variations to suit your daily needs. Feel strong and still, like a great mountain, and be aware of the firm ground beneath your feet.

1. Stand tall, with your ankles and big toes together, then squeeze your stomach inwards and feel your chest lift and open.

2. Keep your breathing smooth and deep. Be aware of your spinal column and lengthen the back of your neck.

3. You could also practise this pose against a wall, feeling the entire back of your body making firm contact with it. This will encourage awareness of a healthy, balanced standing posture.

The mountain pose makes the body feel light and free as a counterbalance to the downward pull of gravity.

Half-moon pose

The half-moon pose gives a tremendous stretch to the sides of the body and defines the waistline area, so if these muscles have become tense or slackened, this pose will tone them. You will also feel a good stretch in the spine because the side curve maintains the natural flexibility of your back. The hips and legs also benefit from this stretch. Choose the arm position to suit your needs. Working with your arms straight is more challenging than holding your elbows. Remember that this is a side stretch, so do not allow your body to fold forwards. In the beginning, your side curve may be a little stiff, but with regular practice you will achieve the moon curve.

1. Stand tall and fix your gaze at a definite point in front of you at eye level. Inhale. Place your arms in position and hold for three deep breaths. Feel your torso lifting upwards.

2. Exhale. Press your hips to the left and curve your body to the right side, holding for three deep breaths.

3. Inhale. Return to the starting position and repeat the stretch on the other side for three deep breaths. Rest and repeat the pose again, feeling your body go deeper into the stretch.

As you gain more experience, you will find that your body is able to hold the poses for longer. This is a sign of progress.

Back arch and forward bend

This combination of a backward arch and a forward bend is the natural complement to the previous pose and can be linked in sequence or done separately. The back arch creates a strong abdominal stretch and the forward bend lengthens the spine and stretches the back of the legs. For optimum benefit, when you are moving from the back bend to the forward bend, keep your body flat and parallel to the floor as far as possible.

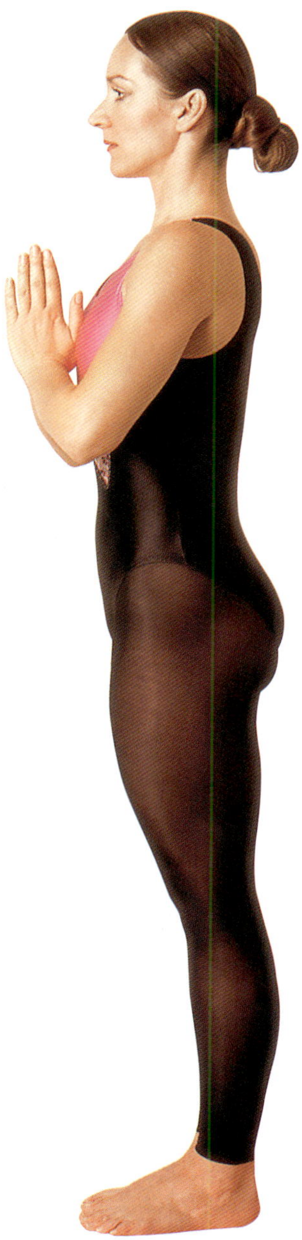

1. Place your palms together at your chest and feel balanced evenly on both feet, breathing slowly and deeply from the abdomen.

2. Inhale while raising your arms up and arching backwards to lift your chest up. Keep your weight on your heels and gently bend your knees if you need to. Hold for three deep breaths while pressing your hips forwards.

3. Inhale. Raise your body into the upright pose and breathe deeply. Inhale. Push your tailbone behind you and, bending from the hips, stretch your body parallel to the floor. Hold for three breaths or more if you can.

4. Exhale. Hang down freely, allowing your arms to drop, or cradle your elbows in your palms, breathing deeply and easily. Roll your body up slowly, to prevent dizziness. Repeat the sequence three or four times.

Tree pose

The tree pose is a beautiful, balancing pose that requires a high degree of mental focus to maintain poise and stillness. Standing on one leg and keeping the body still is a real challenge. This pose develops and enhances your powers of concentration.

1. Stand upright and focus on a single point.

2. Raise your left foot and place it on top of your left thigh. If this is too difficult, place your left foot flat, high on the right inside thigh.

3. Place your palms together at your chest and breathe deeply, keeping your body very still. Feel your right foot firmly rooted into the earth. Hold your body still, just like the trunk of a tree.

4. Breathe deeply, then move your arms upwards, like the branches of a tree, and experience the power of being still in a perfect balance: harmony of body, mind and breath. Don't worry if you wobble and lose your balance, as this is part of your growth.

Repeat the pose and see what happens. Repeat on the other side. Gradually increase the time that you hold the pose and aim for a one-minute balance on each side.

Child pose

The child pose is a soft, forward bend, which places the spine in a release position, easing pressure on the spinal discs. It is practised after back bends to rest the body and can be used at any time during your practice when you feel that it is appropriate. You can also place your palms on the soles of your feet to create a closed energy circuit. As your head rests forwards, it encourages increased blood flow to this area. You can place a cushion or two under your buttocks if your knees are stiff and can also rest your forehead on a soft cushion. This is a wonderful pose for people who experience back problems and helps the spine to realign itself.

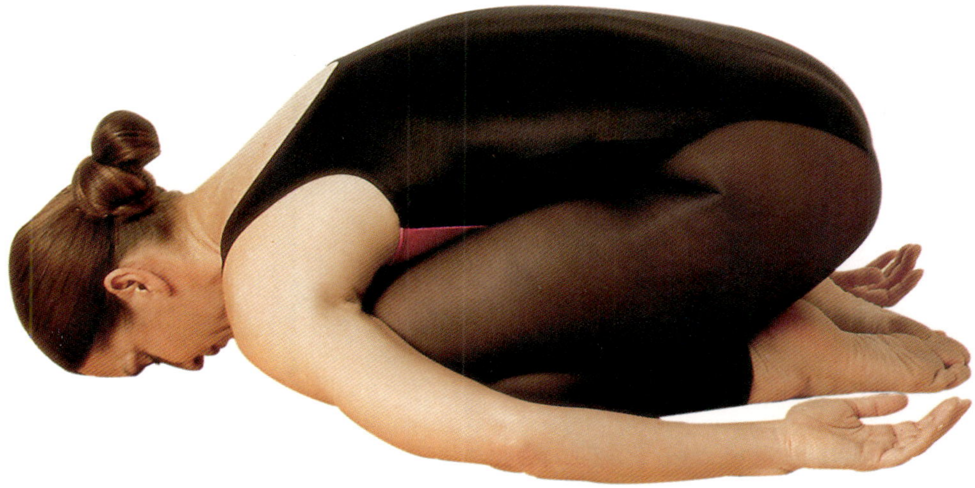

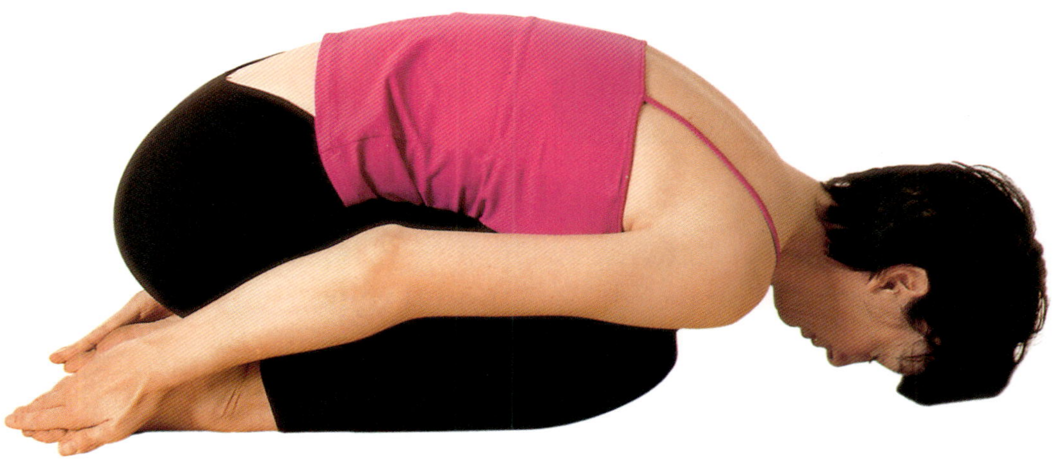

Cat stretch

This stretch, as well as the leg variations, really keep the spine flexible and strong. Cats, who are known for their lithe bodies and quick reflexes, have very long spines for their size.

A

1. Kneel on the mat on all fours, making sure that your knees are well protected. Begin to curl your spine like a cat's arched back. Exhale. Lower your head and let it hang freely. Round your back until you feel a stretch at the back of your shoulders and lift your stomach towards your spine. Hold, breathing deeply for three breaths.

2. Inhale. Raise your head, pointing your chin very high. Feel your pelvis tip backwards, creating a flexible curve along the entire spine. Hold for three breaths and repeat a few times. Rest in the child pose.

B This version increases the stretch and flexion of the spine and involves balancing.

1. Kneel on a mat, with your hands placed flat and your arms straight.

2. Inhale. Extend your right leg backwards and raise it upwards.

3. Lift your head up and hold for three deep breaths.

4. Exhale and lower your leg, bringing your head as close to your right knee as possible. Hold for three deep breaths.

Repeat on the left side.

When you first try this sequence, your head and knee may be a few inches apart, but, with practice, they will touch. Do this pose three times on each side. Rest in the child pose until your spine feels relaxed and soft.

Reclining stretch

This reclining pose really gives the abdomen and thighs a good stretch and frees tension from the pelvic area. The chest is also opened, which develops the full, diaphragmatic breathing that is the goal of your practice.

1. Sit on a mat, with both legs straight in front of you.

2. Bend your right leg and place your right foot close to your right hip, with your toes pointing backwards.

3. Bend your left knee and place your left foot on your right knee.

4. Lean to your right side and place your right elbow on the mat. Inhale. Lean to the left side and place your left elbow on the mat. Stay here for a few breaths as the release begins to occur.

5. Inhale. Lower your head backwards and hold for a few breaths. This may be enough in the beginning. If you can go further, lower the top of your head to the mat and breathe deeply.

6. Exhale. Release your head, move your back as flat as possible onto the mat and raise your arms above your head, holding your elbows. Stay in this final pose for as long as feels comfortable.

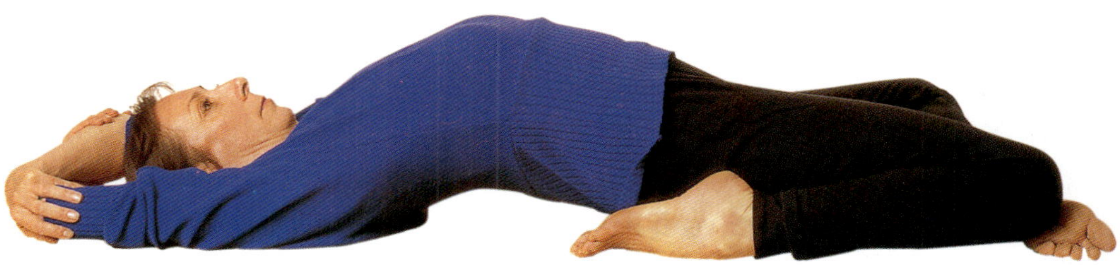

Come back slowly, using your elbows to raise your body, then fold your body forwards and rest. Repeat on the other side. See the advanced variation for deeper body work.

Side splits

This pose increases blood flow to the organs of the pelvic area and opens the hips to free them of tension. The leg muscles are stretched and the sciatic nerves are toned. During the forward bends, the spine is stretched and stiffness is relieved.

A

Place your legs as far to each side as you can comfortably reach. Hold your body very tall as you are sitting, and keep your pelvis lifted in the forward direction. Place your arms in a comfortable position as you feel your body begin to open up. Breathe deeply and slowly.

B

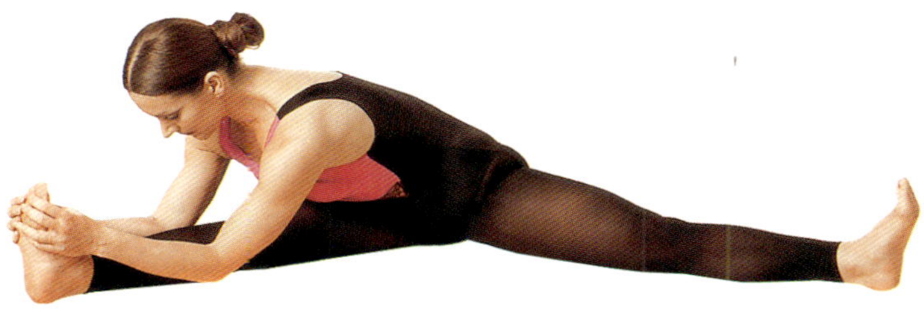

Inhale and reach to your right foot. Exhale, bring your body towards your right knee and surrender to gravity. Breathe deeply and soften your body as you sink deeper into the pose. Hold for as long as you can.

Inhale. Raise your body up and turn to your left leg. Exhale. Reach over your left leg, repeat on this side and hold. Inhale and raise your body up.

C

Exhale, bend forwards and either extend your hands towards your toes or simply let them rest in your comfort zone. Remain in the forward bend for as long as you can, then inhale. Raise your body upright and rest in either the child or relaxation pose.

This is a deep stretch for those who are not used to it, but progress is rapid once you begin. Be brave and don't give up.

Standing stretches

Triangle

The triangle pose is the basis for a series of standing leg stretches that benefit the entire body, especially the legs, hips, spine and chest. These poses relieve stiffness in the joints and muscles and strengthen weak ankles.

1. Stand sideways on your mat, with your feet wide apart and arms extended at shoulder height, with your fingers stretched and palms facing the floor. Turn your right foot 90 degrees to the right wall.

2. Exhale and begin to extend your body sideways to the right. Extend your right hand to hold your ankle. Breathe smoothly.

3. Inhale. Raise your left arm above your head and look upwards. Hold your stillness for three or four breaths.

Inhale. Raise up your body up and repeat the pose on the left side.

Reversed triangle

This pose has the same qualities as the triangle, with the addition of a wonderful spiral twist that increases the flexibility of the whole body.

1. Begin as before, with your feet apart and arms extended. Turn both feet to the right wall.

2. Inhale and rotate your body to the right.

3. Exhale and reach down with your left hand to hold your right ankle.

1. Inhale. Rotate your body to the right.
2. Exhale. Turn your head upwards and stretch your right arm upwards. Hold the pose for 30 seconds, feeling the twist occur in the lumbar area of your spine.
3. Inhale. Raise your body to assume the starting pose and repeat on the other side.

With practice, you will be able to rest your hand flat on the floor near your foot.

Hamstring stretch

This pose works the legs, creating a long stretch for the hamstring muscles. Because there is a forward bend, the spine and shoulders also benefit.

1. Point both feet to the right, clasp your fingers together behind you, squeeze back your shoulders and lift your chest. Inhale. Lengthen the front of your body and lift your arms.

2. Exhale. Bend forwards and bring your head to your right knee, raising your arms high behind your back.

3. Hold the pose, while deep breathing, for 30 seconds.

4. Inhale. Raise your body upwards, with your hands on your hips.

5. Exhale and arch your body into a back bend, squeezing back your elbows to open your chest.

Repeat on the left side.

Warrior lunge

This pose deepens the work of the legs and hips. It eases stiffness in the neck and expands the chest.

1. Step forward with your right leg - hands together.

2. Inhale. Bend your right knee into a lunge, keeping your knee directly above your right anklebone to protect the cartilage from strain.

3. Exhale. Stretch your arms upwards and raise up your head to look at your hands. Hold for 30 seconds.

Repeat on the other side.

Flat-back squat

This pose gives the legs a good stretch, tones the hips and lengthens the spine. As it is an inversion, blood flow is increased to the head.

1. Stand on the mat with your feet apart. Inhale and raise your arms to the side. Exhale. Bend forward from the hips until your body is parallel to the floor. Inhale and hold still. Exhale, bend your knees and sink your hips towards the floor, keeping your body parallel with it. (This is a real challenge to hold because your legs are taking the strain.) Sink deeper into the squat, then hold your ankles, roll your head downwards and exhale.

2. Slowly push your hips upwards and straighten your legs, keeping your chest as close to your thighs as you can.

3. You can repeat this sequence as many times as your body wants. To rest after this pose, kneel on your mat, with your arms extended in front of you, and relax.

Chair pose

This pose tests the legs and keeps the knees and ankles strong by releasing tension. It also enhances balance and helps you to feel well grounded in your body.

1. Stand with your feet hip-width apart and your arms outstretched at shoulder level. Make sure that your shoulders remain directly above your hips.

2. Exhale. Lower your hips downwards until they feel level with your knees. Only lean forward if you have to, otherwise try to keep your body upright. Stay in this position for 30 seconds or more. Inhale and raise your body

Extra challenge: repeat the pose with your heels lifted as though you were wearing high-heeled shoes. This refines your balance and heightens your concentration skills.

Standing bow

This elegant pose creates a powerful arch in the spine and opens the working shoulder while challenging your balance and concentration. Aim to hold this pose in complete stillness for one minute. Start with both feet together in the mountain pose.

2. Exhale and begin lifting your back leg upwards, to a comfortable height. Lower your left arm, palm facing downwards, and stretch out your fingers. Focus your eyes on a definite point.

   Hold the pose for as long as you can without losing your balance. Inhale and raise your body up to assume the starting position, with your knees together, and repeat for the other leg.

1. Pick up your right foot, hold the inside ankle and raise your left arm straight above your head. Squeeze your knees together.

Standing split

This pose works the legs by toning and stretching the muscles and ligaments. It increases blood flow to the brain, opens the hips and helps the spine to retain its natural alignment.

1. Make a pyramid shape by standing with both feet together and hands placed shoulder-width apart.

2. Exhale and raise your right leg as high as you can, keeping your left knee long and straight. Your hips can twist, but try to keep both shoulders level. Hold for five to six deep breaths, then change sides.

Flat-back stretch

This pose extends the back of the legs while flattening the back and helping to refine spinal posture. Be aware of keeping the back of your neck long and straight. You can also turn this pose into a squat by bending your knees and holding for a few moments.

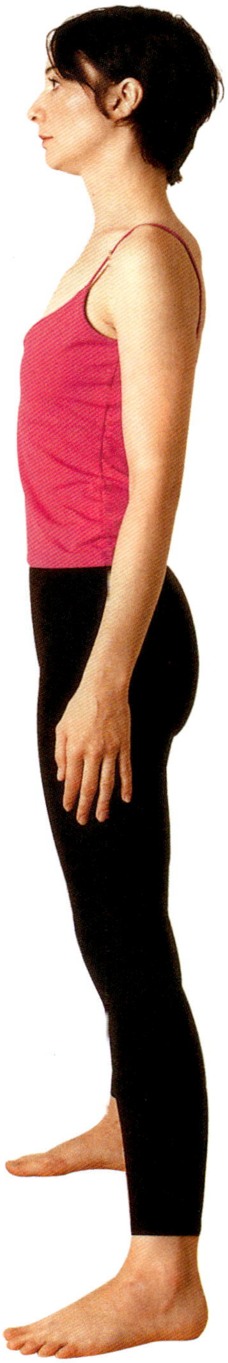

1. Stand with your feet far apart and your hands on your hips.

2. Exhale and bend forwards from your hips, keeping your body as flat as possible. Hold, using deep breaths, and return on an in-breath.

Repeat with a knee bend.

Pyramid

This pose helps to energise the body and is especially good for toning the legs and strengthening the ankles. It eases shoulder stiffness and brings fresh blood to the brain while also resting the heart.

1. Stand with your feet apart and bend forwards, placing your hands flat on the ground.

2. Inhale and walk your hands forwards until you feel the stretch in your legs. Keep your feet flat on the mat and both elbows straight. Your neck should stay long and your breathing deep. Try to rest your forehead on the mat.

Reverse pyramid

This pose stretches the hamstring muscles fully and increases blood flow to the body and head. Tension is released from the spine by the inverted curve and neck stiffness is eased.

1. Stand with your feet apart and your hands on the floor a shoulder-width apart. Inhale and turn your hands backwards.

2. Exhale. Begin to make small walking movements with your hands and see how far they will reach behind you. You will feel the work at the back of your legs. Remain in the pose for three deep breaths. Inhale and reach a little further back with your hands. Hold and relax in the pose.

Repeat this once again, using deep breathing, then lower your body into the child pose and rest peacefully.

Head-to-knee stretch

This pose stretches the legs and keeps the spine flexible. It also works the muscles of the arms and shoulders. As you are lying down, gravity exerts negligible pressure, so the body can release deeply stored tensions from the system. This pose might prepare you to do the splits one day.

1. Lie on your back on a mat and bring both feet together. Inhale and raise up your right leg as high as possible, keeping your right knee straight. Hold your leg with both hands. Exhale. Gently bring your leg a little more into the stretch.

2. Inhale and prepare to exhale. Raise your head towards your knee and hold this stretch for as long as you want. Repeat on the other side. During this pose, you may bend your knee to bring your head to your leg, but only bend it a little. Breathe evenly as you hold the pose and feel your body relaxing peacefully.

Maltese cross

In this pose the entire spine experiences a powerful twist, which increases blood flow to the area and stimulates the flow of cerebro-spinal fluid to the spinal cord and central nervous system. All twists have this effect on the body.

1. Lie on your back on a mat, with your feet together. Place your arms at shoulder height, palms downward, in the shape of a cross.

2. Inhale. Raise your right leg to 90 degrees and hold, keeping your knee straight.

3. Exhale. Lower your leg to the left side, hold and breathe deeply. Make sure that you keep your right shoulder blade in contact with the mat.

4. Inhale. Raise up your right leg and then lower it. Repeat on the other side.

Plough

The plough pose nourishes the blood vessels of the spinal column, the spinal nerves and the back muscles. It keeps the spine flexible and tones the abdominal muscles, while relieving all of the body's organs from the effects of gravity. The shape of this pose resembles the ancient plough that our ancestors used to plough the fields with.

Caution: women are advised not to practise this pose during the first three days of their monthly cycle.

1. Lie on the mat, with your feet together, your knees bent and your palms pressing down near your hips.

2. Inhale and bring your knees close to your chest.

3. Exhale. Swing your hips off the floor, pushing into your hands for support.

4. Inhale. Let your feet rest on the floor above your head and breathe easily. You may prefer to support your spine with your palms.

Remain in the pose for as long as your body feels comfortable. To unwind from the plough, simply place your palms flat on the mat and roll down as slowly as you can. Relax deeply as your body settles and breathe easily.

Shoulder stand

The shoulder stand is also called the 'all-body pose' because it benefits the whole body on many different levels. It is an inversion, so it counteracts the effects of gravity. Most importantly, it massages the thyroid gland at the front of the throat that affects all of the other organs. Pressure is released from the legs and blood flow is increased to the upper body.

Caution: women are advised not to practise this pose on the first three days of their monthly cycle.

1. Proceed in the same way as with the plough, with your hands holding your back. Inhale. Bend your knees and point them upwards.

2. Exhale. Slowly unfold your legs and lift up your spine with your hands.

3. Inhale. Straighten your body as you straighten your legs and hold the pose for three to five minutes, using slow, deep abdominal breathing.

To come down, just reverse the previous moves by lowering your legs behind your head, placing your hands flat on the mat, rolling your body very smoothly downwards and then resting while enjoying the benefits of this pose.

Fish pose

The fish pose acts as a counter-pose to the shoulder stand, which involves a deep neck bend. The fish arches the neck and spine to balance the area and expands the ribcage, making more space for the lungs and heart to function at full capacity.

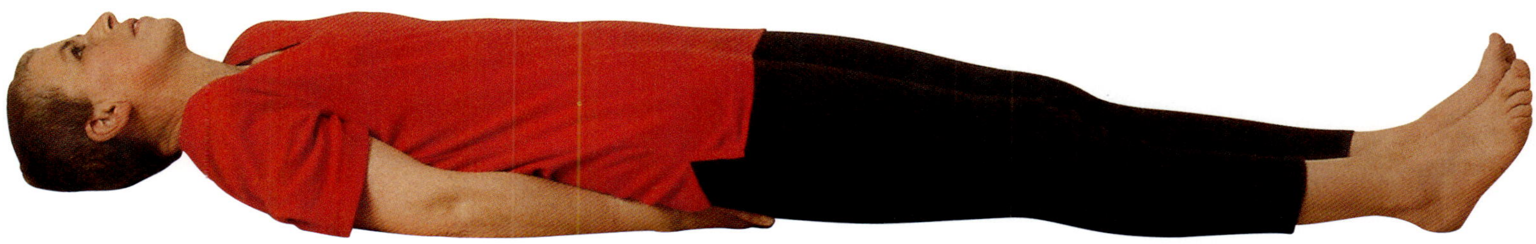

1. Lie on your back, with your arms straight, placed under your body with your palms facing the mat. Your elbows should be straight.

2. Inhale. Push into your elbows and raise your chest off the floor. Exhale. Lower your head back and place the crown of your head gently on the mat. Hold this pose for half the length of time that you held the shoulder stand, breathing steadily.

To release, slowly slide the back of your head downwards and bring your arms to your sides. You can gently roll your head from side to side to ease your neck.

Back-bend poses

Diagonal bridge

The diagonal bridge is a good way to strengthen the back muscles as a preparation for more intense work. It tones the leg muscles, massages the thyroid gland and eases tension from the neck.

Lie on your back and bend your knees to bring your feet close to your buttock muscles. Begin this pose with your feet a hip-width apart, then progress to work with the feet together, which requires more strength.

1. Inhale. Relax your tailbone and sacrum completely and bring your awareness to this area of the lower back.

2. Exhale. Lift up your pelvis to create a diagonal line from knees to shoulders, then place your arms on the same line of symmetry. Hold for one minute, then roll down slowly and relax.

Easy back arch

This easy back arch prepares the spine for more work, expands the chest and can be used as a warm-up exercise.

1. Kneel on the mat with your knees a hip-width apart. Inhale and rest your fingertips on the floor, behind your hips.

2. Exhale, squeeze your shoulders back, lift up your chest and point your chin upwards. Remain seated on your heels. Hold the pose for as long as you feel the benefit in your spine.

3. To release, exhale, fold your body forwards and rest in the child pose, with your head on the mat, breathing smoothly.

Cobra pose

The cobra pose imitates a snake raising up and spreading its hood to strike. This wonderful pose stretches the spine, massages the organs and develops the chest.

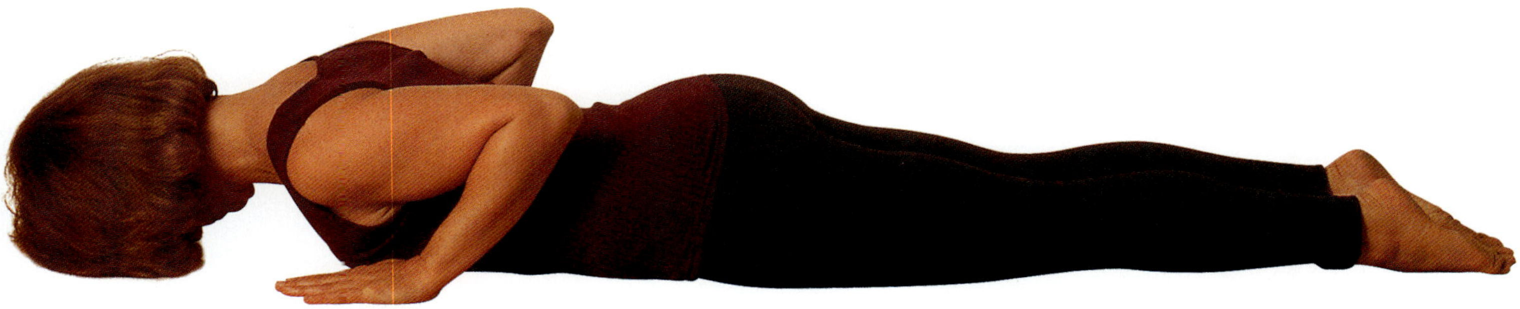

1. Lie on your front, resting on your forehead with your feet together. Inhale. Place both palms down flat, near your armpits.

2. Exhale. Raise your head slowly, then continue arching upwards, keeping your elbows bent and your stomach on the floor. Hold for six deep breaths and keep looking steadily upwards.

Exhale. Lower your body slowly, release your arms, turn your head to one side and rest. Repeat two or three times, then relax.

Bridge

The bridge pose increases spinal flexibility, stretches the shoulders and prepares the body for the wheel.

1. Lie on your back on the mat, with your knees bent and your feet a hip-width apart. Inhale. Reach to your feet and hold your ankles. (This may be tricky in the beginning, but proceed anyway until you can hold them.)

2. Exhale. Raise up your hips as far as they will reach and create an arch with your body. Keep your neck long, with your chin pressed into your throat. Hold and breathe deeply.

To release, let go of your ankles, lift up your heels, roll down your spine very slowly and then hug your knees to your chest.

As you gain more expertise in this pose, practise with your feet and knees together to increase the challenge for your back muscles.

Half-wheel pose

The half-wheel pose requires balance, co-ordination and a flexible spine to achieve, and is a preparation for the full-wheel pose.

1. Lie on your back and prepare by doing the bridge pose. Inhale and place your palms under your shoulders, with your fingers pointing towards your feet.

2. Exhale. Press upwards, onto the crown of your head, and hold for the pose for as long as is comfortable.

To release, tuck your chin forwards, bring down your arms, raise your heels and roll down your body slowly. Hug your knees to your chest and rest.

Wheel pose

In the wheel pose, the spine experiences a powerful arch. According to Yogic texts, a flexible spine preserves youthfulness and energises the body, which is another benefit of the back bends.

1. Perform the stages leading into the half-wheel.

2. Exhale. Press on your hands and straighten your elbows as much as you can. Use your legs to help to raise your body into the wheel. Breathe deeply and hold for as long as possible.

3. Inhale. Slowly bend your elbows and lower your body, releasing it onto the back of your head, then roll down slowly.

Hug your knees to your chest and then rest in the relaxation pose.

Half-locust pose

The half-locust pose strengthens the lower spine, tones the abdominal organs and benefits the reproductive system. It increases blood flow to the heart, as well as cardiovascular capacity. At the end of the pose, you will feel that your heart has pumped to its maximum capacity.

A

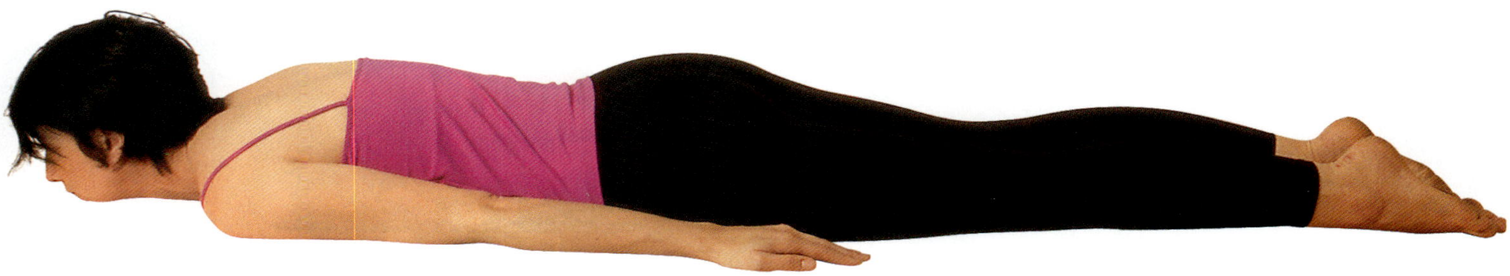

1. Lie face down on the mat, resting on your chin on the mat, with your arms at your sides and your legs and feet together.

2. Inhale. Raise up your right leg and hold, breathing deeply.

Repeat on the other side, then rest on your cheek and relax.

B

1. Exhale. Place your palms flat on the mat near your shoulders and place your left foot under your right shin for support. Hold while breathing deeply.

2. Inhale. Lower your legs and rest for three deep breaths.

Repeat on the other side, then rest until your heart rate slows down.

Full locust and variations

The locust really makes the back muscles strong and healthy, encouraging good spinal posture. The organs are massaged and blood flow to the spine is increased.

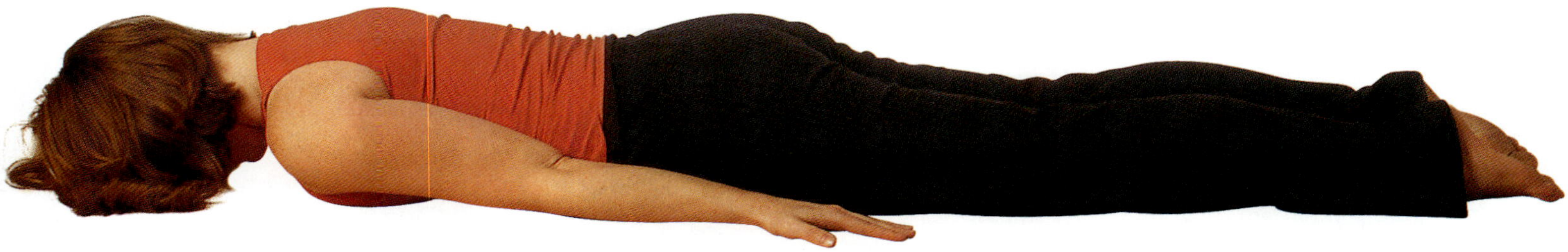

1. Lie face down on the mat, with your feet together and arms straight at your sides, palms facing down.

2. Inhale. Press into your palms and raise up both legs. Keep pressing onto your forehead.

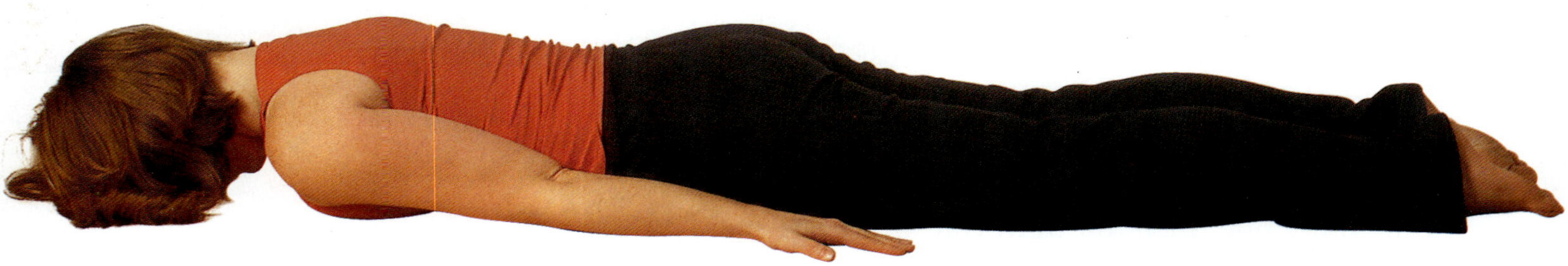

3. Exhale. Lower your legs and breathe deeply.

4. Inhale. Press into your palms and raise your body upwards to hold the position.

5. Exhale. Lower your body and take a few deep breaths to prepare for the full pose. Inhale. Raise your body and legs at the same time while looking upwards. Remain in this position for three or four breaths, then relax slowly onto the mat and rest till your heart quietens down.

Stick pose

This pose resembles a straight stick or rod and challenges every muscle in the body simultaneously. It strengthens the arms and legs and tones the abdomen.

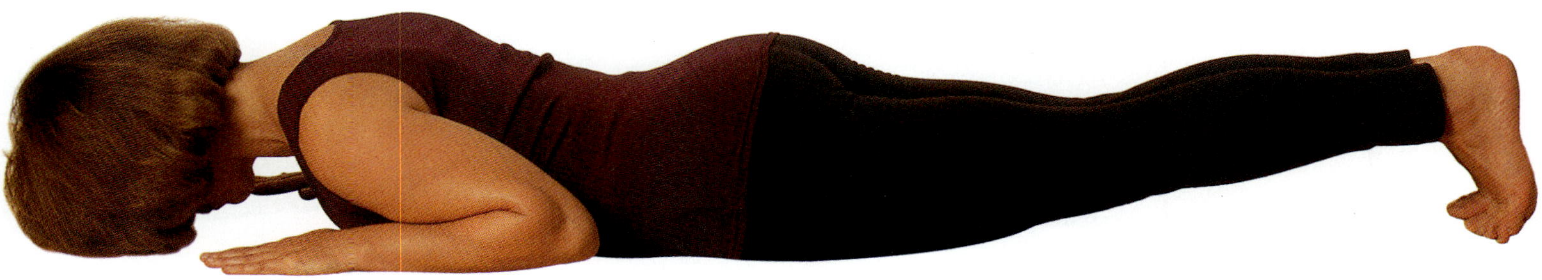

1. Lie on your front, resting on your forehead, place your palms and elbows flat on the mat and tuck under your toes, legs together. Inhale. Tighten your legs and press on your arms.

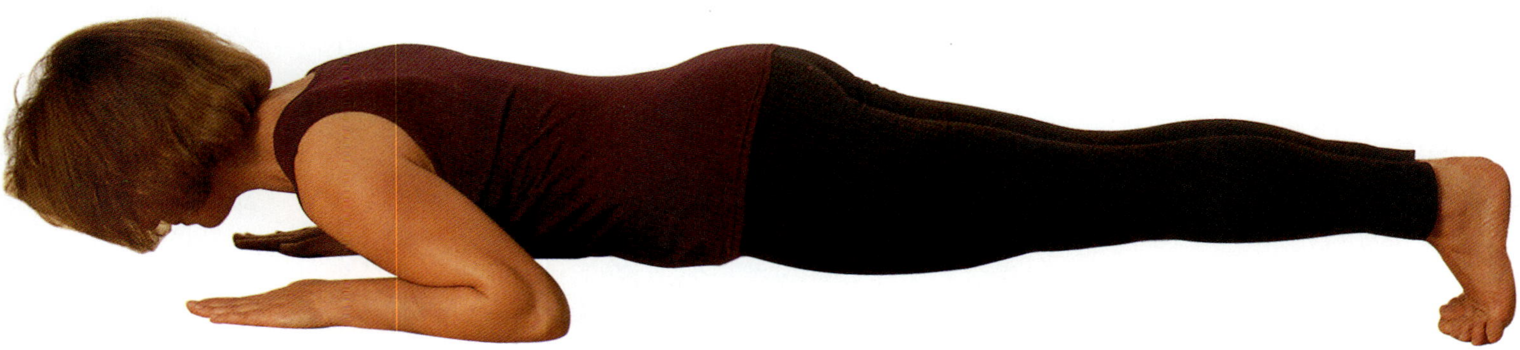

2. Exhale. Raise your body off the floor and keep it very straight. Make sure that your neck is long. Hold the pose for three breaths.

Release and relax your arms and then turn your head to one side.

Bow pose

The bow pose is so named because it resembles the curve of an archer's bow. You will experience more benefit if you rock the pose gently from side to side to increase the organic massage. The balance is on the stomach, which keeps the gastric fire strong and helps to eliminate fat. The chest and shoulders benefit and the spine is energised.

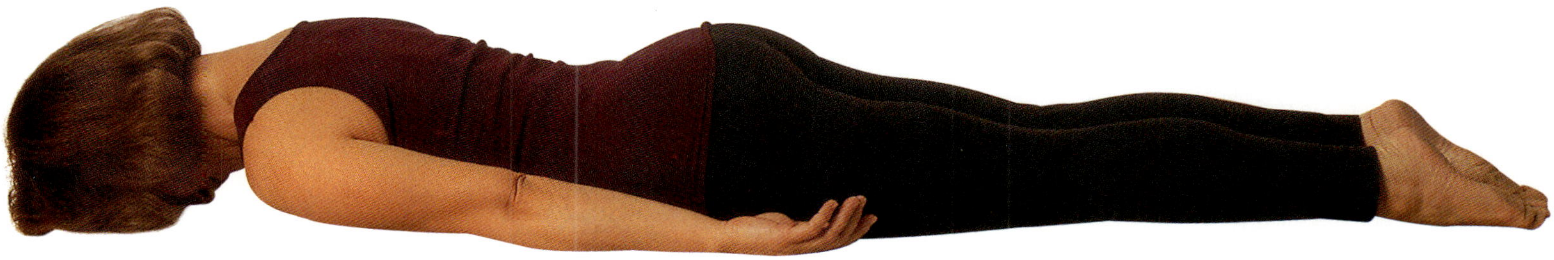

1. Lie flat on the mat and relax completely, breathing deeply.

2. Inhale. Bend your knees, hold your ankles and lift your head.

3. Exhale. Raise up your chest and lift your knees off the floor. Hold for a few breaths, then roll down and relax.

Repeat the pose and gently rock from side to side. Inhale. Rock to the right. Exhale. Rock to the left a few times, then roll down and rest or do the child pose as a counter-pose for the back bends.

Half-camel pose

The back arch of the half-camel and full camel poses help the spine. The deep chest expansion of the pose energises the respiratory system. Tension is released from the neck and shoulder area and the entire front of the body is stretched.

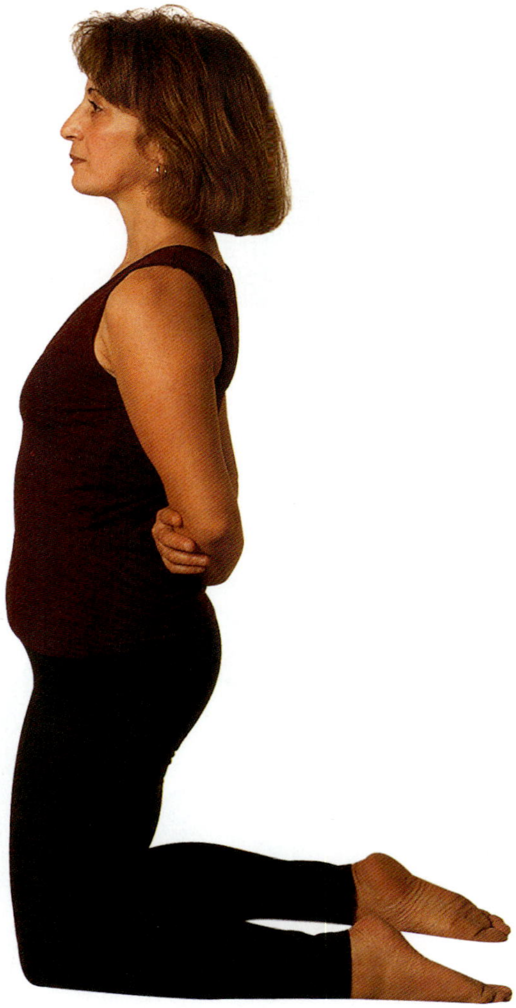

1. Kneel on the mat, with your knees a hip-width apart, and clasp your elbows behind your back. Inhale and gently press your hips forwards.

2. Exhale. Lower your head backwards and let your spine arch backwards. Breathe smoothly as you hold the pose and continue to press your hips forwards.

To release, inhale and raise up your body. Exhale. Sit down, lower your head, relax your arms and rest in the child pose, with your head down. Practise the half-camel until you feel confident that you can do the full pose.

Full camel

1. Inhale. Kneel on the mat, with your feet and knees a hip-width apart, and place your palms flat on the soles of your feet.

2. Exhale. Press your hands onto your feet and lift your hips upwards.

3. Inhale. Press your hips forwards, lifting up your chest. Exhale. Arch into the back bend and roll back your head while looking up.

Remain in the pose for three deep breaths, then release into the child pose. In the beginning, lower-back stiffness may prevent you from arching very much, but with a little practice you will achieve the full pose.

Forward bends and stretches

After the back bends, it is important to balance your practice with forward-bending poses to restore your body to its natural alignment. Learn these poses and incorporate them in your practice.

Half-leg forward bend

1. Sit on the mat with your legs in front of you. Inhale. Bend your left knee and place your foot on your right thigh (half-lotus). If this is too much, let the sole of your left foot rest on the inside of your right thigh.

2. Exhale. Stretch your arms upwards and lift your spine.

3. Inhale. Slowly lean forwards, keeping your body in a long line

Exhale. Rest your head on your knees and hold your foot. Hold for as long as you feel the benefit, then repeat on the other side.

Seated forward bend

An important and beneficial pose to include in your practice, the seated forward bend rejuvenates the spine, reduces excessive fat around the abdomen, tones the liver, kidneys and stomach and stretches the entire back of the body, from the heels to the back of the head.

1. Sit on the mat with both legs straight in front and feet together. Inhale. Raise your arms above your head and lift your body as high as possible.

2. Exhale. Slowly lean forwards and let your hands rest where they reach naturally. Bring your head towards your knees and breathe deeply in the pose.

Remain in the forward bend for as long as your body enjoys the stretch. In the beginning, you can bend your knees to soften the pose. Feel the whole weight of your body creating the stretch naturally, with the help of gravity. Remember to breathe slowly and deeply as your body sinks deeper into the bend.

Rabbit pose

The rabbit pose looks easy, yet you will feel a lot of changes happening when you practise it. (Women can use this pose instead of the shoulder stand.) The rabbit pose stimulates the glands of the neck and brain, stretches between the shoulders, tones the organs and stimulates the reflex points of the feet.

1. Kneel on the mat with your knees and feet together and tuck under your toes. Inhale. Reach down and hold your heels firmly.

2. Exhale. Lower the crown of your head, close to your knees, and rest it on the mat.

3. Inhale. Lift your hips and point your tailbone upwards. Let the weight roll gently to the back of your head.

Hold the pose while it is comfortable. Your breathing will be shallow due to the forward pressure. Rest in the relaxation pose.

Deer pose

The deer pose is a gentle pose (like the animal itself) that offers all of the benefits of the child pose, with additional chest expansion and shoulder-toning. Blood flow is increased to the upper body and head. Keep your palms pressed together.

Kneel on the mat, with your knees and feet together and your head resting, forehead down, on the mat. Inhale. Place your palms together behind your back. Exhale. Raise your arms as high as possible and point your fingers towards the sky. Hold for six deep breaths. Release your arms and rest in the child pose.

Half-inclined plane

In this pose, angles are created by the arms and legs as the body balances firmly on the hands, heels and feet. The front of the body is stretched, the legs and arms are challenged and the back-support muscles are engaged. This pose prepares your body to practise the full inclined plane.

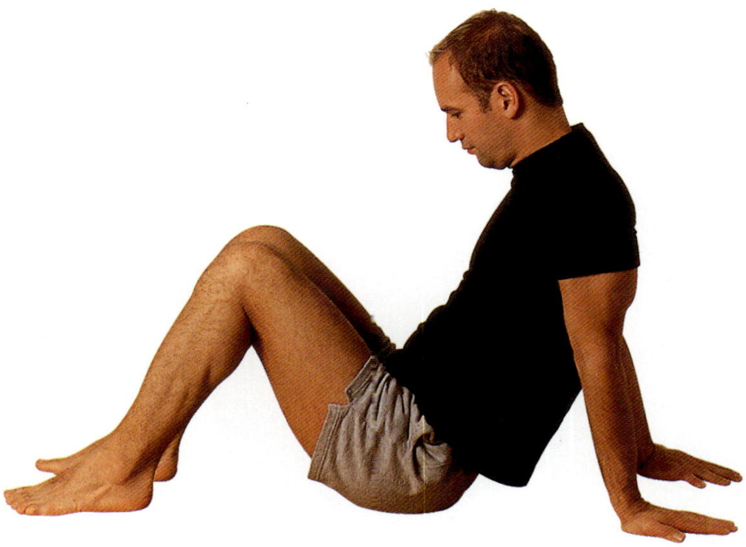

1. Sit on the mat, with your knees bent and feet together. Inhale. Rest your palms flat beside your hips, keeping your elbows straight. Your fingers can point either backwards or forwards to work the wrists.

2. Exhale. Lift your hips high and stretch back your head. Make your body as parallel as possible to the floor.

Hold for three deep breaths, then release and repeat a few times. To make this pose easier in the beginning, place your feet a hip-width apart.

Inclined plane

The full inclined-plane pose requires more strength and precision to hold with straight legs. You will feel the challenge that this involves.

1. Sit upright, with both legs straight in front of you and your feet together. Inhale. Place your hands flat beside your hips and draw your shoulders back

2. Exhale. Press firmly into your feet and raise up your body, keeping your knees straight. Try to keep both feet flat on the mat or balance on your heels. Keep your hips raised for as long as you can, then lower them and relax on your back. This is quite strenuous.

Mermaid twist

Twist poses are a wonderful way of keeping the spine flexible, but the body must be well warmed up. The mermaid twist eases the body into a good rotation that stretches the spinal nerves, increases blood flow to the spine, tones the kidneys and massages the pericardium.

Kneel on the mat, then sit on your left side, with both feet on the right.
Inhale. Place your left hand on the mat near your left hip and place your right hand on, or near, your left knee.
Exhale. Rotate your body to the left and hold, breathing deeply. Stay in the twist for three deep breaths, then repeat on the other side.

Relaxation pose

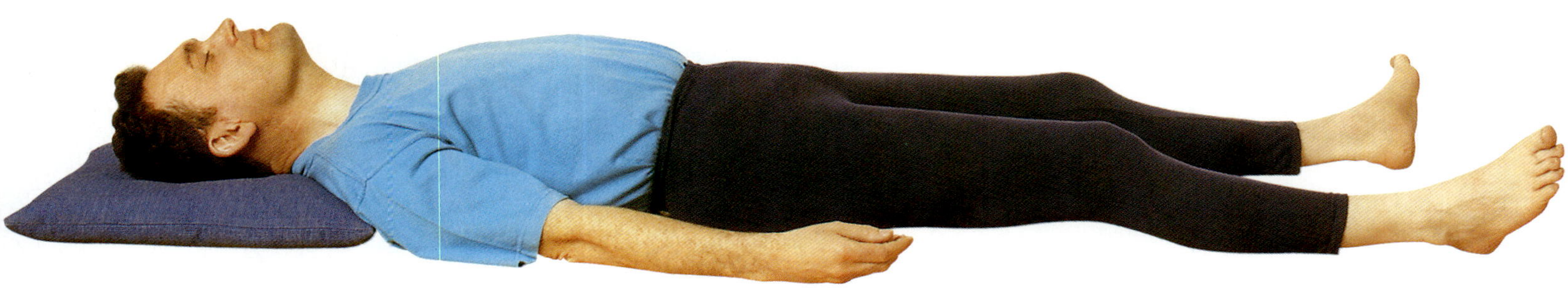

Remember to practise the relaxation pose at the end of your session, however long or short it has been. The relaxation pose brings your body and mind back to objective reality in a smooth transition, and safely prepares you to continue your daily activities.

Yoga for the office

This sequence has been designed specifically with working people in mind to help to alleviate the side effects of sitting or standing for long periods of time. There are many simple and effective techniques that, if used regularly, will release accumulated tension.

It has been suggested that the human body would benefit from a postural change, stretch or bend at least once every 15 to 20 minutes. Experiment with these movements, discover some of your own and create your own therapy from experience through awareness. These simple movements will help you to maintain well-being at your workspace. A chair with arms can enhance the range of movements you may experience.

Eye exercise

Computer-vision syndrome is now widely acknowledged and may affect your vision through exhausted eye muscles. Blinking quickly is a very good way of releasing tension from the delicate muscles of the eyes.

Sit tall in your chair and blink your eyes quickly 50 times. Do this once an hour for each hour that you are working at a keyboard and progress to 100 blinks.

At the end, simply close your eyes and breathe deeply till you feel your temples and forehead muscles relax. (See the *tratak* section in the meditation chapter for more eye exercises.)

Forward bend

This exercise stretches the lower back, releases pressure on the sacrum and tailbone, massages the lungs, relaxes the shoulders and increases blood flow to the head.

Sit back in your chair, with your lower back touching the back of the chair.
Inhale. Separate your knees and stretch your body upwards.
Exhale. Lower your head, round your shoulders and roll your body down as far as you can, hanging your head gently and resting your chest on your thighs.
Hold and then roll up your body slowly.
Repeat this a few times to feel like a ragdoll, flopping and totally letting go.

Hands and feet

1. Flexing and pointing the hands and feet gives the ankles a chance to release tension and helps the circulation to flow through these constricted areas better.

2. Also try rotating your ankles and wrists clockwise, and then anti-clockwise, to maintain their flexibility.

Twist

Twists are a wonderful way of energising the spine and increasing blood flow to the area.

Inhale. Place one hand on the back of the chair and the other on the arm or seat (right side).

Exhale. Turn and twist your body to the right, holding for three breaths.
Repeat on the other side.

Leg tuck

This is a superb way of shifting your body weight while keeping your spine and pelvis supported, resting one leg and energising the system.

Remove your shoes and tuck one foot underneath your hips. Sit for about ten minutes, then change legs. You may need a cushion for your ankles if the chair is unyielding.

Shoulder release

This helps to prevent drooping shoulders and a rounded chest and eases stress on the shoulders.

Inhale. Tuck your elbow behind your head.

Exhale. Press down and hold the stretch for as long as it feels remedial.

Repeat on the other side. Also try three or four movements in a row on each side.

Working with a partner

When you practise Yoga with a friend or partner, your ability to observe the symmetry of the human body will be developed and this in turn will help you to become more sensitive in your own practice.

You will begin to observe the lines and planes of the body in relation to the specific pose that is being worked. In the lunge pose, for example, the arms must be straight and parallel to the floor, something that a partner will be able to assess and gently adjust if necessary.

Another benefit of partnerwork is using your body weight gently to assist the person to move into a deeper position. Remember to ease the body and never to use force. Always make the adjustments when your partner is exhaling.

It is good exercise consciously to breathe together during this work. You will also notice where your partner's body is holding tension, and this will in turn guide your own practice.

Child pose – spine stretch

For this pose, you will need some cushions or folded blankets to protect the head, knees and feet.

Kneel in the child pose with your arms stretched forwards. Gently lower your tailbone onto your partner's and slowly roll onto their back with your arms sideways. Pressure may be increased by pushing from the feet. Remain here for as long as you are both comfortable – ask your partner whether they need less or more pressure – and then change places.

Flat-back stretch

It can be difficult to achieve a flat spine on your own in this position, so here is a simple way of releasing back tension and giving the legs a good stretch at the same time. You may also do this with your palms flat against the wall, using your hands to ease the back into a flat plane. Practise this a few times in turn and note the improved flexibility that comes with repetition.

Side lunge

When you work this pose together, keep your back and shoulders touching, chins in line with the shoulders and arms stretched and parallel. Remember to keep the knee bent above the ankle to prevent strain. Hold for three deep breaths on each side.

Flat-back squat

This assisted bend works with your combined body weights to give the back a fine stretch, at the same time as strengthening the legs and toning the hips. Aim to keep your bodies parallel to the floor and bring your hips level with your knees. Inhale. Hold each other's wrists and lean forwards to flatten your backs. Exhale. Lower your hips and lean back gently. Hold, using deep breaths. Inhale. Rise up and relax.

Triangle

This really works the sides of the body, the legs and hips. You may find that your body won't go as far as usual with a partner, however. This is good, because it keeps the pose in a purely side alignment

1. Stand back to back, with your palms together or holding wrists if there is a difference in arm length. Inhale. Turn your head to the same side.

2. Exhale. Lean sideways and lower your body to the floor – you can rest your fingertips on the floor or simply hold. Repeat on the other side.

Assisted diagonal lunge

When you practise this lunge with a partner, you can feel the strong stretch of the diagonal line and can keep legs and hips from rounding.

1. Aim to keep both hips level.

2. And a straight top arm.

3. Return and repeat on the other side.

Double diagonal lunge

You will feel the challenge involved in holding the perfect symmetry of this pose, using your partner's back as a support.

1. Inhale. Stand back to back as on page 105 and turn your heads to the side.

2. Exhale. Lunge to the side and rest your palms or fingertips on the mat. Keep as much back, hip and shoulder contact as possible.

3. Raise up your bodies and repeat on the other side. Rest.

Balancing trees

This is a partner version of the Tree Pose on page 49, and the same stages should be followed.

Standing on one leg alone is a difficult pose, and even with a partner it can be tricky adjusting to each other's wobbles. Once you have established balance, work on keeping the pose very still, stretching the 'branches' of the tree upwards and sending the 'roots' deep into the earth. Breathe together evenly.

Kneeling-forward bend (1)

In this pose, the top person lends their weight and the person underneath creates the stretch by holding their wrists.

1. Inhale. Kneel behind your partner's back and rest your hands on their shoulders.

2. Exhale. Lean your body onto your partner's back and exert a little pressure.

3. Inhale. Straighten your knees and let your whole weight rest on your partner's upper back. Your partner should hold your wrists to create the stretch.

Breathe deeply, then release and change places.

Kneeling-forward bend (2)

In this variation, the person on top experiences a spinal stretch and chest expansion. It is also very relaxing.

1. Inhale. Squat against your partner's back.

2. Exhale. Lean back and raise your hips – keep body contact.

3. Inhale. Raise your arms over your partner and they will continue the stretch by gripping your wrists. Hold, breathing together, then gently slide down and rest.

Advanced poses – *asanas*

These poses have been chosen both to inspire and to show the potential progress that can be made with regular practice. Advanced *asanas* are a natural progression, which you may achieve spontaneously or with guidance from your instructor.

Reclining kneeling pose

This full pose will occur when the front of the body has released all tension. If your knees come off the floor, revert to the half-leg pose described earlier.

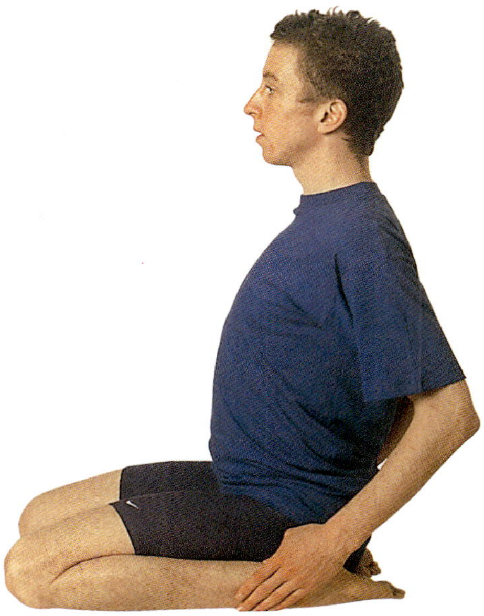

1. Inhale. Sit on your heels, with your knees and feet apart, and hold your ankles.

2. Exhale. Lower your body back and downwards, resting firmly on your elbows. Arch your chest and allow your head to roll back.

3. Inhale. Rest on the crown of your head and remain in this position until your body begins to release its tension.

4. Exhale. Release your head, bring your back flat onto the mat, bring your arms above your head and hold your elbows, breathing deeply, for as long as you can.

Raise your body slowly, using your elbows, and rest in the child pose.

Half-spinal and full spinal twist

The spinal twist is a progression from the mermaid on page 96. Prepare for the full pose by practising step 2 for a few weeks until your body is ready for step 3 and ultimately step 4.

1. Sit in the mermaid pose, then place your left foot over your right knee.

2. Inhale. Place your left hand on the mat behind you and press your right elbow on the outside of your left knee. Rotate to the back shoulder.

3. Bend your right arm under your left knee.

4. Catch hold of your back hand. Breathe deeply as you enjoy this wonderful stretch, then repeat on the other side.

Deep forward bend

This is an extension of the seated forward bend (see page 91). The stretch becomes deeper with the addition of the arm position.

1. Inhale, with your feet together, straight knees and your arms above your head.

2. Exhale. Bend forward, relax and breathe deeply.

3. Inhale. Clasp your fingers behind your back. Exhale. Raise your arms as high as possible, feeling the rotation in your shoulders and bringing your head towards your knees.

Raise and relax your legs.

Extended wheel

This pose is exactly as it sounds. The subtle shift of weight from one side to the other is part of the skill involved learning this pose. You will need to have patience with this one.

1. When you have mastered the wheel (page 81), learn to balance with one leg extended upwards.

2. Then repeat on the other side.

Headstand bridge

This pose, a combination of the headstand and the wheel, creates a magnificent arched balance. It can also be done with alternate leg-raising for refined balance.

Crow balance

This balance requires pure concentration and a single, pointed gaze, like a crow's. The hands mimic the feet of the bird, and your body balances on your arms.

1. Inhale. Place your hands on the floor, with your fingers spread for balance.

2. Exhale. Place your knees on your upper arms and slowly lift your hips up. Stare at a point 2 feet (about 60 centimetres) in front of you.

3. Inhale. Raise your feet off the floor.

4. Hold for three breaths.

Come down and rotate or shake your wrists.

Side crow

This pose refines your balancing abilities even further.

1. Inhale. Place your hands on one side, a shoulder-width apart.

2. Exhale. Begin to lean forwards, resting your legs on your arm.

3. Inhale. Lift your feet and hold the pose for three breaths, then relax as before.

Full locust pose

This supreme pose usually takes many months of practise to achieve. Raising the legs to this height involves pure strength in the back and stomach muscles, as well as precision timing.

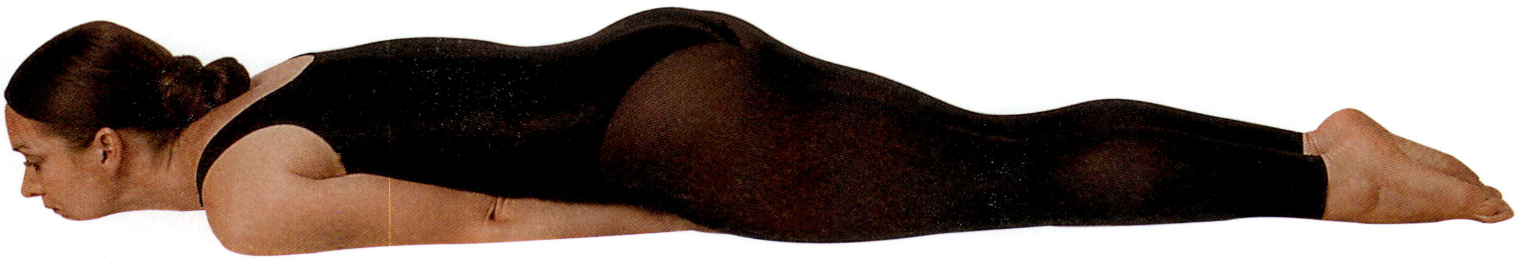

1. Inhale. Lie on a mat resting on your chin and place both arms under your body, keeping your elbows straight and palms down so that you can push into the floor with your arms.

2. Exhale. Raise both legs quickly and hold the pose while breathing deeply.

3. Inhale. Bend your knees and point your toes towards your head.

Lower your legs, release your arms and rest until your heart quietens.

Meditation

What is meditation? Meditation is 'Raja Yoga', or royal Yoga, the Yoga of the mind.

Yogas chitta vritti nirodahaa.'Yoga is transcending the mental waves of the mind.'
SAGE PATANJALI

Meditation is an ancient practice used to enter deep levels of consciousness and experience the nature of the true self without being disturbed by the busy complications of daily life. It is not necessary to isolate yourself in a Himalayan cave to meditate. Meditation, like Yoga, can be experienced in any quiet place where you will not be disturbed.

Meditation encourages the mind to be quiet, and in that stillness the inward perception experiences unity (Yoga), inner peace and, ultimately, self-realisation that is beyond description.

'When the Knower, the experience of knowing and the knowledge become one – that is Yoga. When the mind, body and breath rest with each other without a separate identity – that is Yoga.'
H H SWAMIJI SATCHIDANANDA

Meditation techniques

Practical techniques are used to train the mind and body to experience stillness, and many physiological benefits are derived from regular meditation. During concentration and meditation, the metabolic processes of the body slow down and the life force – *prana* – is able to flow freely and nourish the body on many levels of consciousness.

Regular meditation has a rejuvenating effect on the mind and body, calming the central nervous system and slowing the brainwaves to preserve precious nervous energy. Many scientific studies have been carried out on people who practise regular meditation, and the physiological benefits are real.

During your meditation, allow your mind to move freely and become aware that you are observing its movements. Don't try to force your mind – simply observe where it is going. Notice your breath and concentrate on quietly observing the mind. You will know when it is time to end the meditation.

You may need to lie down in the relaxation pose to rest your muscles or write in your journal the experiences that you felt during the practice.

Some people choose to focus their minds on a sacred word during meditation, as this gives them an anchor and helps to slow the thinking process. Experiment and find which techniques work best for you.

Lotus pose *Padmasana*

This pose is used for meditation because the body is safe, with a low centre of gravity due to the broad, pyramid-like base. Notice the left foot resting on the right thigh, which affects the flow of blood to the body and calms the system. This is the traditional meditation pose.

Sitting cross-legged is another option, as long as this is comfortable and you are able to remain still during the meditation. Any physical movement will automatically disturb the mind.

Kneeling pose

Kneeling is another effective way of practising meditation because of the effect on the blood's circulation, which calms the body. However, most people need much practice before they are able to remain in these two poses for more than ten minutes.

The most important aspect of your chosen meditation posture is that your spine should be tall, allowing the energy to flow freely during the sitting. Poor posture would both hinder your progress and be uncomfortable. You might like to sit on a cushion, with your back against a flat wall, and feel the support during your meditation.

Candle-gazing – *Tratak*

Tratak – gazing at a candle or sacred object – has long been used to develop concentration and lead the mind into a state of inner perception and tranquillity. It focuses the mind on a single point and has the effect of calming the many thoughts that rise and dissolve, like the waves of the ocean. In fact, we have all practised this unconsciously before: we call it day-dreaming, when the eyes are staring into the distance and we are not paying attention to the here and now.

Tratak is conscious day-dreaming, with the added benefit of the brain's sight receptors receiving pure light directly from the candle through the eyes.

Candle-gazing – *Tratak*

1. Sit in the pose of your choice.
2. Place the candle or sacred object at eye level.
3. Begin to focus on the object without straining your eyes.
4. Breathe smoothly and evenly.
5. Slowly widen your eyelids and try not to blink.
6. Continue this, then close your eyes.
7. You may see an image between your eyebrows, at the third eye.
8. Keep your eyelids closed and hold your attention on the third eye.
9. Open your eyes and continue this process of concentration until you are ready to meditate with your eyes half-open or closed.

Caution: remove contact lenses and glasses when you practise this technique.

Diet and lifestyle

A true Yogic diet would, by its very nature, be a vegetarian one. Remember the first *Yama*, the *Ahimsa,* which advocates non-violence – this clearly means not killing any creature in order to sustain one's own existence. This is not a new precept and can be found in many world religions and philosophies.

It has been suggested that fasting the body for one day each week rests the organs and allows the body to eliminate waste material from its tissues. A one-day fast simply means not eating any solid food for 24 hours and instead drinking diluted herbal teas during this period. For a person whose constitution will not tolerate a total fast, thin vegetable soup is recommended.

In our busy, technological, modern world, in which speed and automation rush us headlong into a confrontation with our host planet, the prevalence of 'fast food' is proving detrimental to human health. Yogic philosophy suggests the following tips for your well-being and natural health.

1. Use only fresh food for cooking.
2. Do not eat food cooked in a microwave oven.
3. Never eat any food that has been processed and stripped of its natural vitality.
4. Avoid all food with additives, food colourings and preservatives.
5. Avoid canned foods.
6. Never eat when you are upset or angry.
7. Eat only when your stomach has digested the previous meal.
8. Never eat when your body is thirsty or drink when your body is hungry.
9. Avoid extremely hot or cold foods or drinks.
10. Eat foods that are naturally in season where you live.
11. Avoid eating and conversing at the same time.

Massage is an important routine to incorporate in your lifestyle. Use warmed almond oil or cold-pressed sesame oil before your morning shower or bath and practise some gentle Yoga while your body absorbs the oil. Massage your body from your head down to your feet.

In the morning, find a quiet time in your routine for some **meditation** and contemplation to allow your inner self to guide your day. Listen to your body and pay close attention to its real needs. When asked about enlightenment, Lord Buddha said, 'Eat when you are hungry and sleep when you are tired'. During your daily walk, ask yourself 'Does this honour my peace or does this disturb it?' and act accordingly.

Health is our birthright, and sickness is simply a sign that our lifestyle has become unbalanced. Yoga practice will reward you with natural health, self-realisation and peaceful well-being.

Index

Where to find out more

Classes with Frances at Natureworks
16 Balderton Street
London, W1
www.natureworks.co.uk
tel: (020) 7629-2809

Sivananda Yoga Centre
51 Felsham Road
London, SW15 1AZ
www.sivanandaYoga.org
tel: (020) 8780-0160

Yoga & Health Magazine
Editor: Jane Sill
PO Box 16969
London, E1W 1FY
www.yogaandhealthmag.com

Credits & acknowledgements

I sincerely wish to thank the following people, who generously and lovingly guided and supported the creation of this book:

Ian Cuthbert
Jennifer Drew
Maurice Nash
Julie Peacock
Antonella Ghironi
Penny Spencer
Jake Fox
Tessa Skola and Alexandra Warwick, for demonstrating the poses.
Karuna Milne, for his ever-present guidance.
Sarah King, for being the midwife to my first book.
Nandi and Shanthi, for their patience and inspiration.
James Boodoosingh, for his love and light.
Om Shanthi.

The pictures on pages 6, 7, 8 and 125 were taken by Sylvia Melder at Ocean Beach, Central Coast, Sydney, New South Wales, Australia.